MONASTIC WISDOM SERIES: NUMBER THIRTY-SEVEN

Christophe Lebreton, OCSO

Born from the Gaze of God

The Tibhirine Journal of a Martyr Monk
(1993–1996)

MONASTIC WISDOM SERIES: NUMBER THIRTY-SEVEN

Born from the Gaze of God

The Tibhirine Journal of a Martyr Monk (1993–1996)

Christophe Lebreton, OCSO

Translated by
Mette Louise Nygård
and Edith Scholl, OCSO

Cistercian Publications
www.cistercianpublications.org

LITURGICAL PRESS
Collegeville, Minnesota
www.litpress.org

A Cistercian Publications title published by Liturgical Press

Cistercian Publications
Editorial Offices
161 Grosvenor Street
Athens, Ohio 54701
www.cistercianpublications.org

This work was originally published as *Le souffle du don : Journal du frère Christophe, moine de Tibhirine 1993–1996* © Editions Bayard 1999 – Centurion.

A second edition was published in 2012 by Bayard: Frère Christophe, *Journal. Tibhirine 1993–1996. Le Souffle du don.*

Biblical quotations are generally taken from either *The New American Bible* (USCCB, 2002) or *The Jerusalem Bible* (London: Darton, Longman & Todd, 1974), whichever accords more closely to the French original.

2 3 4 5 6 7 8 9

Library of Congress Cataloging-in-Publication Data

Lebreton, Christophe.
[Souffle du don . English]
Born from the gaze of God : the Tibhirine journal of a martyr monk (1993–1996) / Christophe Lebreton, OCSO ; translated by Mette Louise Nygard and Edith Scholl, OCSO.
pages cm. — (Monastic wisdom series ; no. 37)
ISBN 978-0-87907-037-3 — ISBN 978-0-87907-673-3 (ebooks)
1. Lebreton, Christophe. 2. Trappist—Algeria—20th century—Diaries. 3. Christian martyrs—Algeria—Tibehirine—Biography. 4. Victims of terrorism—Algeria—Biography. 5. Tibehirine (Algeria)—Church history—20th century. 6. Notre Dame de l'Atlas (Monastery : Tibehirine, Algeria) I. Title.

BX4705.L42475A3 2014
271'.12502—dc23
[B] 2014008648

We had accepted within ourselves the sentence of death,
that we might trust not in ourselves
but in God who raises the dead. . . .
In Him we have put our HOPE.
(2 Corinthians 1:9-10)

—entry for Thursday, December 15, 1994

Contents

PREFACE TO THE PRESENT EDITION

by Henri Teissier, Archbishop Emeritus of Algiers

In a letter to his parents of February 1992, Brother Christophe wrote: "Yesterday brought me a nice satisfaction. In the vineyard Ali said to me: 'So, one can really tell you're beginning to know how to prune.' To do it well you have to look beyond the branch that's apparently dead. You have to see the invisible fruit, still to come. This fruit is for everyone, and so we must work together."[1] All of Christophe's rich interiority may be found in this brief statement: his fellowship with the Tibhirine farmers that shared the work of the monks in the monastery garden; his humility as apprentice who had to get used to working the land, after arriving in Algeria with his law degree ("you're beginning to know how"); his knack for passing directly from everyday concerns ("pruning the vine") to a meditation rooted in his daily reading of the Gospel ("the invisible fruit of the branch"); his desire to work with his neighbors and friends of Tibhirine ("we must work together"); and, finally, his glance turned toward the future ("you have to see the invisible fruit, still to come").

1. Marie-Dominique Minassian, *Frère Christophe Lebreton, moine de Tibhirine* (Bégrolles-en-Mauges: Éditions de Bellefontaine, 2009), 144. This is the spiritual biography of Brother Christophe, written after conducting a wide survey of his family members and making a thorough study of all the texts available. M.-D. Minassian wrote her doctoral dissertation on the spiritual message of Brother Christophe.

We should add that this text also reveals the poetic density innate to all Christophe's writings, and the very natural spiritual depth that contributes to the richness of his journal and his exchanges with those close to him. We see these qualities present in this other brief statement, taken this time from the journal: "This afternoon Mohammed is inviting Christian and me to have coffee at his house. He's just finished laying down the floor in the foyer of his house and in the bedroom. The future of faith comes to meet us in this shared story" (October 30, 1994). This "shared story" is the very precise and important stage in a young and simple family's life that allows it to leave the ancestral home where life as a couple is being crushed by the preceding generation and numerous assorted relatives. For such a young couple, building their own home means giving themselves the possibility for honest, mutual intimacy and for assuming the responsibility of raising their own children. However, for the spiritual person that Christophe is, this specific event concerning one of the workers associated with the monastery takes its place in the "sacred story" that is being written around the monastery, through the human growth of the neighboring families. For him, this "story" is shared by the monks and their neighbors alike: "The future of faith comes to meet us in this shared story."

In these two little episodes I recognize all the dimensions of Christophe's personality, just as I knew him when I used to go every two or three months to the monastery of Our Lady of Atlas as archbishop of Algiers. I used to go simply to meet with the monks, or to accompany a group making a retreat with them. He was "Tibhirine's gardener of the moment," and at the same time the youngest of the monks, the most straightforward of them, but also the poet and true man of the spirit among them, as the journal shows. I had the opportunity to chat with him when he showed us his garden or introduced us to his Algerian associates. I would also meet him in chapter, to which Prior Christian invited me each time I was traveling through, or in the personal interviews that Father Christian asked me to have with each of the monks at those moments when the community was going through its gravest trials. I also had occasion to admire his spiritual message when, at my request, he held a day of recollection for the bishops of North Africa, of whose conference I was then president. But I have to admit it was when I discovered his journal that I truly came to appreciate—and with great emotion—the depth of his interior dialogue with the Lord, a dialogue that was always marked by his attention to the persons and events surrounding him, as well as to the persons and events of our Church and of Algeria. This is the reason why I am very grateful to Éditions Bayard for taking the initiative of this new edition so as to put at the disposal of a greater public the message of Brother Christophe.

As the situation started getting more serious around the monastery and in Algeria at large, the reflections Christophe entrusted to his journal likewise reached an even more impressive depth. After a serious incident, when twelve bodies belonging to terrorists were exposed for all to see in the neighboring town of Medea, Christophe notes in his journal: "On his return from Medea, and still shocked by what he had seen, Mohammed said to me: 'The worst thing is that Muslims did this to Muslims. This is terrible.'" He then adds: "In Rwanda [in this same year of 1994], Christians did it to Christians. Indeed, the faith is being tested, shaken" (August 20, 1994).

This same capacity of making the connection between concrete events and their spiritual references made him reflect as follows on another dramatic incident in 1994: "To drink the blood of the Lamb places us in one camp: that of the victims. Our young neighbor, Ben Yussef Zubir, died yesterday, because an army truck hit the car he was in. An innocent victim joined to you, our paschal Lamb. I should like to intervene, to stand in the breach and try and stop these killings that go on every day. It must be done by a truer, more total form of engagement, in prayer" (October 11, 1994). Here he connects an event, the death of a neighbor, to the biblical reference that gives it meaning: "the paschal Lamb." On the situation of the monastery, caught between the army and the terrorists, he ponders thus: "Perhaps it's not enough to say that we don't have to choose between the powers that be and the terrorists. In fact, every day we have to make the concrete choice of those Jean-Pierre calls 'the little people'" (March 14, 1995).

All the friends of the monastery at Tibhirine are grateful to the scriptwriters and actors of the film *Of Gods and Men* for having given a great public access to the monastic life of the Tibhirine community—its prayer, its daily work, its fraternal bonds, and its relations with the surrounding Muslim world. Some of the actors, like Michael Lonsdale in the role of Brother Luc, succeeded wonderfully in entering into the life of the monk they incarnated. We think also of Jacques Herlin in the role of Father Amédée, one of the two survivors, now deceased. Nevertheless, in order to bring out the dramatic character of the decision taken by the monks to remain faithful, the director chose to depict a marked tension within the community between those who, like the prior, Christian de Chergé, embrace the risk incurred, and those among the monks who hesitate before such a difficult choice. The film thus shows Brother Christophe as the one who had the greatest difficulty in embracing the grave risk the community is running, and the possibility of martyrdom.

This is not what I recollect from my dealings with Brother Christophe and the monastery. Naturally, they had to make a difficult decision. But they weren't the only ones to do so. We should recall the context. The whole of Algerian society and the Algerian Church were living under this threat. Christophe's journal enables us to enter into the spiritual atmosphere that accompanied the monks' decisions. I myself can attest to this interior attitude, since at Father Christian's request I twice met with each of the brothers. I did not feel in them the anxiety the film portrays. To be convinced of it we have only to recall the following reflection from Christophe's journal in 1995, after the violence had already taken a toll of eight of our brothers and sisters, both religious and priests: "I don't think anyone among us is much concerned with his own life. This greatly clears the way before us as a community!" (August 23, 1995).

All of Christophe's very numerous references to the Paschal Mystery in the journal go in the same direction. Witness this text of August 1994: "The mail hardly ever arrives here any more. The bridge has been blown up. The forest is burning. There is no water and it is hot and then here, you know, killing happens here a lot. A glance at history shows that failure obviously dominates, unless from your cross your hand writes in us, in me too, illegible love" (August 4, 1994). Such spiritual realism is applied by Christophe also to the celebration of the Eucharist as "sacrifice of the cross": "What makes the liturgy is the paschal event. This didn't occur in church but on a cross that had nothing liturgical about it. What was involved was a murder and the blood of an innocent man and his tortured body. I await for adoration in spirit and truth." Already in 1993, two days before the first visit of the terrorists to the monastery, Christophe wrote: "The impossible resolution, yes, I have made it: received from You. Love obliges me: This is my body: given. This is my blood: poured out. May it be done unto me according to your word, may your gesture pierce me through. And this resolution—that is yours: it's infinitely beyond me. A resolution stronger than death" (December 22, 1993).

We should also take into account another evolution in Christophe's life. It's clear that, ever since his arrival in Tibhirine, he became involved in very rich daily relations with his Muslim neighbors, especially those who worked in the garden with him. But it's quite surprising to discover that it was only in 1994 that he wanted to join the monastery's Muslim-Christian prayer group (the *Ribât es-salâm*[2]). He will do so as a particular response to the

2. "Bond of peace."

death of Marist brother Henri Vergès, assassinated in the Kasbah on May 8, 1994. This brother, a profoundly spiritual person, was a member of the Ribât. Impressed by his death and his message of life, Christophe on this occasion petitions the prayer group as follows: "I sense something like a secret appeal from Henri [Vergès] to come join you in this kind of mission-presence. I am attracted not by ideas or by a system but by the place of the Ribât such as Henri lived it. To be sowers of love just where we are."[3]

Christophe is not interested in an "Islamic-Christian dialogue" that would be nothing more than an abstract encounter, cut off from everyday life. He often refers to his encounter with his Muslim neighbors, but on another register. He wanted to live a spiritual life that embraced his Muslim friends rather than engage in any heady discussion on the two confessions. This is, for example, what he wrote in his journal in 1994: "In the house of Islam—in the present state of its Algerian structuring (!)—it's probably not opportune to present oneself as the house across the street—structured differently. It's better to be the Body of your Presence resolutely and simply, to be simply there in a relation of love, vulnerable, exposed" (March 20, 1994). And again: "Our Gospel mission: to live the Good News of our relation with Muslims. Today we're going to work in the vineyard: You, planted here in this land of Algeria; you: bear in us fruits of friendship" (March 29, 1994).

With Christophe's journal we have in our hands the day-by-day report of the events that marked the Tibhirine community from August 1993 (four months before the first visit to the monastery by the terrorists) until March 19, 1996 (seven days before their abduction). This testimony is given us by a deeply spiritual person who was also a poet. Christophe was the youngest monk in the community. He touches us as much by the sincerity of his

3. Minassian, *Frère Christophe,* 214.

Christian confession as by the expressive quality and depth of his monastic and spiritual life. He touches us also by the very concrete color of his "confessions." I venture the word because they remind me of the confidences that Saint Augustine recorded fifteen centuries earlier, precisely here in Algeria.

The famous "Testament" of Father Christian de Chergé will abide as one of the great spiritual texts of the twentieth century. In it he expresses himself both in his own name and in that of his community. Brother Christophe's journal brings us a witness of the same proportions. For almost three years Christophe connects his personal testimony to the concrete events of his own community, of his region (Tibhirine and Medea), of the Church of Algeria and of Algeria itself. All who were touched by the tokens of fidelity given in the film *Of Gods and Men* will find in Christophe's journal an overwhelming testimony of what one of the monks of the community was living through during this period. "I am like everyone here and like our neighbors: tired, weighed down. Indeed, the story of men is a grave thing. The work of God is the true labor of a monk. I love performing it here. This place is holy. A place of true adoration in the Breath of the Nazarene." These lines were written on January 2, 1994, one week after the first forced entry by the terrorists into the monastery.

Tlemcen, Algeria
September 22, 2011

A LONG LOVE POEM

PREFACE TO THE FIRST EDITION

by Dom Armand Veilleux

"I love you." These words, underlined, ring out like a refrain throughout Brother Christophe Lebreton's journal. In the purest Cistercian tradition, Christophe is madly in love with God. After all, have not several twelfth-century Cistercian Fathers left us commentaries on the Song of Songs? That "I love you" broke forth from him one day while he was studying in Tours, like a cry that came from the very depths of his being. It transformed his life completely. That cry, which in turn became poetry and music, remained in him until his last breath.

In him, that mad love for God was neither romanticism nor rootless energy. He was embedded in everyday monastic life, with its sometimes prosaic challenges, in his contacts with brothers and neighbors, in his intimate relationship with his family and his friends in Algeria and elsewhere. He called this journal a "prayer notebook." It begins on August 8, 1993, a few months before twelve Croatian workers were assassinated at Tamesguida, near his monastery at Tibhirine, and stops with the entry of March 19, 1996, a few days before the seven brothers at Tibhirine were abducted. It allows us to follow what not only Christophe but the whole community of Tibhirine lived through day by day, during this period that was so full of tragic events.

Christophe came from a wonderful family. His journal reveals a beautiful relationship with each member of his family. Toward the end of this period his father died, a few months before the drama at Tibhirine. He arrived at his father's deathbed just before he died, and wrote with great respect in his journal the words that his father confided to his mother before he died: "Tell Christophe that I have doubted much and yet always believed." Christophe recognizes himself in this demanding faith. Had he not written the following prayer a year before? "Facing death, tell me—Love—that my faith will be steadfast. Suddenly, I am terrified of believing" (December 1, 1994).

While the infernal circle of death is tightening around them, the monks of Tibhirine grow together in a union with God that is comparable only to their fraternal union. Mutual understanding did not go without saying in such a gathering of strong temperaments. Christophe himself has problems overcoming his aggressiveness; in choir, where he is often cantor, the spontaneous prayer that he sometimes blurts out is: "I'm fed up with the office!" It is also moving to read from his pen gems like the following: "In chapter yesterday morning, a very soft light shone about us: we were 'all gaze' listening to one another, listening to you" (March 13, 1995); or: "I don't think anyone among us is much concerned with his own life. This greatly clears the way before us as a community!" (August 23, 1995).

The Tibhirine community had gotten rid of the greater part of their large property after Algerian independence, and had afterward worked out a cooperative plan with a few neighbors to exploit the small piece of land that was left. Christophe, who was responsible for this work, was in almost daily contact with the neighbors and was friends with several of them, whose names and reflections grace his journal. Once, when he returns from a journey, he writes, for example: "What a joy to meet Mohammed, Ali and Moussa" (February 12, 1994).

He did not have much knowledge of spoken Arabic or of Islamic studies, but in the story of his friendly relations with the neighbors of the monastery and his workmates, he reveals the ordinary Algeria, the country of "the little people," in all its beauty and freshness, so different from the country of the military and the extremists. In Christophe's dialogue with his workmates, where he collects all their words of wisdom and deep faith, we have "inter-religious dialogue" in its everyday form, which is the richest and most important.

The nearly three years covered in this journal were years of unheard-of violence in Algeria. From the first pages of the journal, we read: "Assassinations in Algiers. After so many others. This journal cannot remain sheltered from this violence. It pierces me" (August 22, 1993). During the months that follow, Christophe does let himself be pierced by the violence. Notes like that recur again and again like a painful litany. The death of missionaries killed during this period is mentioned every time with great sobriety of words. He had friendly relations with almost everybody. The death of thousands of Algerians, who were victims of the same violence, upsets him just as much, and he is no stranger to the violence in other countries, such as Bosnia, or the slaughter in Hebron.

Like all the other brothers at Tibhirine, he systematically refuses to choose sides with one camp or the other in this mad spiral of violence. He sees the same power of Evil at work in the Islamist terrorist actions as in the bloody reprisals by the forces of order. Refusal of all violence does not mean rejection of those who are violent. Christophe declares his disagreement with a so-called democrat who places herself in the line of the eradicators, and who describes on television her project for a society where there is no room for the other side.

Christophe has great sympathy for Brother Luc, the doctor in the community, who treats whoever is sick or wounded without concern about his or her ideological, political, or military affiliation. The "brothers of the mountain," as they call the Islamists at Tibhirine, come as well. Christophe notes with a smile how Luc, at the beginning of Holy Week, asks them not to come this week unless, that is, they are very tired (April 10, 1995).

This journal is also a long answer to the question that is often asked: Why did the monks at Tibhirine stay at the heart of this violence? They were certainly not unaware of the dangers. More than once they asked themselves the question, explicitly and in community: should they stay or not? To remain seemed to them a demand of fidelity, to God first of all and to their vocation, but also to the people of Algeria, and to the Algerians at Tibhirine in particular. The solidarity that they had knit with the little people must not be betrayed. When Moussa says to Father Christian, the prior: "If you leave, you deprive us of your hope, and you take away from us our hope" (January 4, 1994), or when Mohammed repeats to Christophe: "You still have a small gate that you can escape through. For us there is no road, no gate!," Christophe writes in the journal: "It is a question of defending far more than a monastery. The mission to the people who suffer opens wide its house of prayer" (December 29, 1993).

To stay is a decision that the brothers of Tibhirine have taken knowingly, and Christophe is openly annoyed when he gets the impression that certain church authorities want to make that decision for them. "Are you also going to leave us?" is the question repeated by their neighbors there and then, making the same question from Jesus to his disciples echo in their hearts.

Christophe even becomes a little sarcastic when the papal nuncio tries to organize a transfer of the monks to the nuntiature. The monks cannot imagine staying anywhere except at Tibhirine, and their neighbors cannot imagine them elsewhere either. "I am not here to defend Christian ideas, an ideological truth that can so easily be exclusive. What remains for us is the freedom of hostages: not the freedom to escape, but the freedom of the person that goes further, breaking through the imprisonment imposed by all violences" (March 23, 1994).

Is this a desire for martyrdom? No. Christophe loved life and wanted to live. That is why the daily contact with the death of persons that were dear to him, and with his own death, which became a steadily more realistic possibility, created no unhealthy desire for death, nor a proud desire for martyrdom.

At the same time, as death gradually becomes less improbable, it is accepted. He loves to quote the lapidary phrases of old Brother Luc, wise and grumbling, who says: "I don't give a damn about death, and I am not afraid of either the terrorists or the police" (March 24, 1994); but who also says at the prayer of the faithful: "Lord, give us the grace to die without hatred in our heart" (December 31, 1993).

Shortly after the Croats were abducted, the monks agreed about a scenario in case of attack: if they were all together at the moment of an attack, they were to stay together. If, on the other hand, the attackers came while the monks were scattered around the monastery, each one was to save himself as best he could. That is why, when six "brothers of the mountain" arrived on Christmas Eve in 1993, Christophe and another brother hid in an empty vat in the cellar of the monastery. There they spent several hours, convinced that they were the only survivors; but then they discovered that their brothers were alive and well, chanting Vigils of Christmas. That event was decisive for Christophe's spiritual development. It was, literally, a descent into death, and a rebirth. It was not easy for him to overcome a feeling of guilt, and a certain anxiety that he had been a coward. But it was also a school of humility that opened him to a greater love of Christ and his brothers, and an ever greater freedom in the face of the death that might come.

He crosses another stage in self-giving when he writes, at the end of 1994: "Oh, if dying could stop and prevent the death of so many others, then I would gladly say with pleasure: Yes, I volunteer" (December 30, 1994). And about a month before their abduction, after having planted a cross in the garden, a gift from one of the last missionaries to be killed, he wrote: "When will it be the hour to be sown—beloved in you—at Tibhirine?" (February 19, 1996).

The last few lines of the journal were written on March 19, 1996, feast of Saint Joseph, but also the anniversary of his consecration to Mary, whom he loved with great tenderness. The last words he wrote were: "I shall walk with a perfect heart." A few days later, the final march toward captivity and death began. His last poem was written in his blood, mingled with that of the Lamb. It is his uninterrupted *"I love you."*

ARMAND VEILLEUX, ABBOT
Our Lady of Scourmont

Chimay, Belgium
January 26, 1999

FOREWORD TO THE FIRST EDITION

by Father Jean-Pierre Schumacher[1]

Brother Christophe's sermons, as well as his poems, had an attraction that was peculiarly their own, appealing by turns to sensibility, imagery, and feelings. We find the same personal traits in his journal of the period between August 8, 1993, and March 19, 1996, which were the last years of our common life at Tibhirine, before the drama that brutally interrupted it on the night between 26 and 27 March 1996.

Christophe has a way of presenting everyday facts that is not dull, neutral, or cold. His narrative is alive; it contains a soul—his own. He tells of things the way he lives them, sees them, and feels them. That is so true that often his writing allows realities to emerge from the depths of his being, giving glimpses of his faith, of his generosity in gift of self, of his attention to God present in all beings and events, of his hope open to the Kingdom, still to come and yet already at work in the humble realities of the present moment and even more beautiful in what may be sensed in the chiaroscuro of faith. Sometimes there emerges with intensity (why not say it?) his passionate love for the Lord and Algeria, to which he dedicated his life. Noticeable also is his concern for the little ones, his suffering in the face of the evil gnawing at social life and sowing so much misery among men. He feels inadequate, but not desperate. Sometimes the intimate

1. Father Jean-Pierre, prior of Our Lady of Atlas after Father Christian, is one of two monks, the other being Father Amédée, who survived the abduction and murder of the seven brothers.

drama that confronted us as community during that period emerges between the lines.

Perhaps one might say that this journal allows the reader to slip into Christophe's manner of contemplating persons and events. No doubt the resulting awareness is more precious and, at bottom, more exact than what would come from an observer who, looking at things from the outside, might make a presentation that would certainly be objective, but also neutral and cold. There is a dimension of warmth and humanity here that stems from a member of the community, one of the flowers of the many-colored bouquet that made it up. In this journal, written with fidelity and care, we are given precise and concrete everyday details that are invaluable when recalling this last segment of the community's history. This journal has another advantage, which is that it discretely reveals the interior of the life of one applying himself, like a diligent and interested pupil, to write in living letters the great history that is written by the very hand of the Master of History. Christophe describes this task in the following terms: "To join words together is real work. It seems to me that I've been hired to do something else: to join the world to you by means of words passing through me. So: when shall I be able to write in all truth the word that Algeria, that all men so severely lack: MERCY?" (09/01/1993).

FATHER JEAN-PIERRE SCHUMACHER
Titular Prior of Our Lady of Atlas

Fez, Morocco
November 26, 1998

PRESENTATION

This journal of 1993 to 1996 is made up of a notebook, and in addition a handful of loose sheets written during Brother Christophe's stay in Fez during May and June of 1995. The other texts he wrote during this period, in particular his homilies and the daybook of the community during Father Christian's absences, are not a part of the journal.

Brother Christophe loved to add little designs to certain pages of his journal. Thus, for instance, in the phrase *I love you* the word "love" is almost always replaced by a ♡. Besides the heart, we have retained a dozen or so other designs, less frequently used, that appear in the journal and illustrate a text or actually replace it, such as † or ☆. As far as possible, too, we have tried to reproduce the graphic originality of the text in its punctuation, spelling, and syntax.

We have left unaltered all quotations and references to books given by Brother Christophe. Passages written in Arabic or Italian have been translated.

At the end of the book, following the journal, we have included a section of unpublished texts from the pen of Brother Christophe (poems, messages to friends, letters), as well as photos that trace his life's itinerary, from early childhood to his life with his brother monks at Tibhirine.

The Atlas community that emerges in this portion of the journal was made up of Father Christian, Brother Luc, Father Amédée, Father Jean-Pierre, Brother Michel, Brother Paul, Brother Célestin, and Brother Christophe, to which should be added the monks residing at Fez in Morocco: Father Bruno, Father Jean-Baptiste, Father John of the Cross, and Father Guy. All of these monks are referred to by the titles of either "brother" or "father," the latter especially in the case of the elders, but in general Brother Christopher simply prefers to call them by their first name.

Tibhirine Journal

1993–1996

1993

This nice notebook, left on my schoolboy's desk on the feast of Saint Christopher, invites me to come, gives me a sign to write inside its enclosure. Without betraying the silence of its pages. One must follow the lines,
listen to what the verticals say
then place the words as they emerge
and develop the sentence
it can move quickly, in a hurry, inspired by a sense that orients it
and pulls it beyond the page
toward the words of another
whose assiduous reader
I am
in this place called a scriptorium.

This big notebook: what kind of writing will fill it?
I shall keep it up.   I beg you.
To transcribe the gift from day to day
You are the friend
it is you who knock
and ask   for shelter
in my home you want to tell
a story
that happens to me
Open up to me you say
my sister
my friend
my dove   my perfect one

To write will be
to open up to me
I opened up to my beloved   but turning his back
he had disappeared.
To write will be
to seek
writing is the wound of one who is sick with love.

Writing: my soul   bursts forth in his Word
(A. Chouraqui,[1] Song 5:6)
Writing is obedience.
In this feast-day book
the miracle may happen
if I do everything well
as the bridegroom says
one should do

As servant I shall fill this notebook
that it may serve to give joy
and a life of covenant.
I am held by the sign
the writing will be crucified
marked by you
my king
the king
it is written

I shall speak my poem for the king
my speech will be neither quick nor brilliant
with no beauty of appearance

1. André Chouraqui (1917–2007), French-Jewish lawyer and writer, born in Algeria. Translated the entire Bible (both the Jewish and the Christian scriptures) from Hebrew and Greek into French from 1970 onward. By his unique manner of translating, he revolutionized the reading of the Bible in Francophone areas. Brother Christophe follows Chouraqui's translation of the Bible in many of his biblical references, and we have followed this in our English renderings.

the words simply
look at you
if you wish
it will be
a notebook of prayer
begun on this Sunday
August 8, 1993
at Tibhirine

[08/09/1993] August 9th.

You present the page to me. How can I utter you?
A great desire devours the words that write themselves: to see you.
This journal gazes on you.
If it might keep to this one thing necessary
To write just what has to be said
To obey the unknown words
today
not to close my heart
to consent to the opening
that obliges me

[08/10/1993] August 10th.

My writing does not aspire to any synthesis capable of transmitting a message, or ideas. I intend rather to just say it. I am the servant-scribe. I shall obey the law of your mouth.

To transcribe a kiss. What an adventure. My writing is all
stirred up at the thought.
The one holding my hand
draws it on beyond words.
I shall write your silence. Without translating.
If anyone has ears, let him hear.
I shall write from above, thus escaping any ambitious project
I have no ambition,
I speak softly.

I shall say what comes to me
from you
and writes itself in me
This writing detaches me
from the world
Who will teach me how to write on earth
as it is in heaven?
This morning, I only put this down
LIFE
(The page trembled, the promised page.)

[08/12/1993] Today (August 12, 93 at Tibhirine) I love you.

No, you ask me for no proof. You believe it infinitely.

It remains for me to fill this writing. To be converted today to what is written between us: binding me to you. And it is you who give the shape of love to my existence. Your *I love you* appeared to me one day.

I have not recovered from it.
I stay next to "this well that nothing can empty"
(Jean-Claude Renard).[2]
Emptied out.
On one All Saints' Day I signed on the official sheet your *I love you.*
What takes place here
is a hidden story,
it is a game of love or nothing at all.

[08/15/1993]

To introduce into the grid of this page
woman
that is what comes to me
on this fifteenth of August.

2. Jean-Claude Renard (1922–2002), French poet.

And the writing is invited to greater humility.
Not to pursue anything. Not to plan anything. Above all
no soaring.
Can one write simply in a silent consent to the gift?
Marian writing is existence that corresponds,
not without anguish, not without pain,
to the Word that finds shelter here
house of flesh
The writing would be dwelt in
not without a certain disturbance to the syntax
or the spelling
The writing would let you be seen, you who come
tireless thirsty loving
The writing: heavy like a pregnant woman
in pain: in labor.

[08/18/1993] The 18th.

It's no trifle to keep a journal. Very tidy? How to do it.

Would you please hold my hand, keeping it from straying or leading it back to the straight line?

Grant I may write rightly.

[08/20/1993] The 20th.

I had to prepare a homily. I gave it today. I feel empty: bereft of the sense of the words that were pronounced just now with persuasion and conviction: "to love" "to pray." They drew strength, light and truth not from me but from the Gospel.

But tonight I have lost their taste. They mean nothing to me.

It was you who spoke them. I look out for them on your lips.

Your eyes invite me to the silence where you form them. I shall keep silent in you.

For your sake to stop writing and set off for the ineffable.

[08/22/1993] Sunday (August 22nd).

I copy this bit from a scrap of writing I found among some other papers yesterday. I had written:

By your strength body and blood cries tears,
I think I am about to be born.
Before me: openness
That's good.
I have only
to follow
at your risk.
Are these words true today?
I live at your risk.
The Woman is the one
who draws me
into this game

(evening)
Assassinations in Algiers. After so many others.
This journal cannot remain sheltered from this violence. It pierces me.

[08/23/1993] Monday.

Yes. To be your body here exposes us to this violence that is not aimed at us for the moment.
Would it not be better if one person gave himself up for this country?
My servant, you say, shall be there † where I am.
One must really follow you.

Monday evening.

Read this by Marie-Alain Couturier[3] *(La vérité blessée* ["The wounded Truth"], p. 180): "What we are, what is most precious

3. Marie-Alain Couturier, OP (1897–1954), was a French Dominican priest, who gained fame as a designer of stained-glass windows and was noted for his modern inspiration in the field of sacred art.

in what each one of us is, what is most inexpressibly ourselves in what we are, does not depend on us. It is given to us."

Are the words in this journal "for giving away"?

[08/28/93] August 28th.

There is already a feast-day gift in this journal; there is: you.

And then: she has come into it. Oh, I am far from not being present, far from forgetting myself in order to make room; but sometimes I can actually write without (too much) glancing at myself.

Can actually write toward you.

Will you teach me how to write for you,
for the service of your heart?

Am I in the process of inventing a mission for myself?

The scribe of the cross is a disciple. He is a child. The world is waiting for the words of this childhood. The Liar is lying in wait to devour them, to pervert them as soon as they are born.

I shall write in the desert.

I shall defend your cause. If your breath takes my hand:
I shall obey your language.

[08/29/1993] The 29th.

To hear you telling me to take up my cross makes me realize that to do that I must let go of what occupies (preoccupies) me, let go of all other things.

Must follow you headlong into your freedom.

[09/01/1993] September 1st.

To join words together is real work. It seems to me that I've been hired to do something else: to join the world to you by means of words passing through me. So: when shall I be able to write in all truth the word that Algeria, that all men so severely lack: MERCY?

[09/05/1993] The 5th.

I lack the diligence to keep this journal, whose aim is basically to test my existence as being a word in the process of writing itself here. In order so to utter you.

Christian has gone away for more than a month, leaving me in a more vulnerable position. Like yesterday, when I "refused a permission." It should only be a matter of defending your will, and thus the freedom of the person who chooses to go through a mediation before engaging in action. W.'s freedom consisted in putting up and thus, I think, taking responsibility.

[09/08/1993] The 8th.

Mulud was in choir yesterday, head crowned with flowers (that he will take off at the end of the office: *Barakha. Aissa. Huya* ["Blessing. Jesus. She"]).

I was moved to feel his hand holding on to my cowl to keep his balance. We prostrate together for the doxologies, which he manages to get out . . . more or less, but he says *amín* with great conviction at the end.

Father Scotto[4] died yesterday in Valence, far from home, far from his own country. He was here less than a month ago. His last words to me ring true: "I'm happy to have seen you." As for me, you know: I really long to see you again.

[09/12/1993] The 12th.

Yesterday, poor and empty after listening to him for a long time, I said to D.: "Do you really believe that something of your life has passed over into me?"

Saying this, I said something that commits me way beyond myself: something that commits you in me and crucifies me.

4. Father Jean Scotto, former Catholic bishop of Constantine, born in Algeria 1913, died September 1993.

And to have written this statement shakes me up and attracts me. I hope it is true.

As far as your Spirit wants to take me. On we go. It's SUNDAY.

If you would only untie my hand
and loosen completely my detached
heart, then I could *write you.*

This detachment is at work, taking its time to do everything well in accordance with your cross.

Do you have in mind you some mission
of love?

[09/18/1993] September 18th.

The destruction of the country continues: attacks, a school burnt at Medea.

There is a place for the cross and for a new people to be reborn.

The voice of Edith Stein[5] (in the refectory): "The spirit of God is meaning and strength. It gives new life to the soul and makes it capable of realizing things that by nature are beyond it, at the same time showing it a direction for its action. At bottom, any demand full of meaning that penetrates the soul with a strength that engages it, is a word from God. There is no meaning that does not have its eternal origin in the divine Logos. And he who makes haste to embrace such a word at once disposes of the divine strength to conform to it" (p. 66 in *The Power of the Cross*).

Encounters in the guesthouse during the last couple of days. Salima lets me see the Good News in action: giving substance, deep joy, serenity, strength, happiness, freedom.

5. Saint Edith Stein (1891–1942), known in religion as Teresa Benedicta of the Cross, OCD, was a German Jewish philosopher who became a Catholic and later a Discalced Carmelite nun. She was martyred at Auschwitz.

Yesterday we had here a woman psychologist from Paraguay and a psychiatrist, Salim. And Maya, a little child: the Gift glimpsed in the exchange. Were not our hearts burning . . . ?

[09/22/1993] September 22nd.

Salima: to be recognized as a woman, a whole and complete person, by God and by others. I will be baptized, I know it, I feel it.

Childhood and the cross. To be born, and the means to be born. Because it is real, because nothing but Mystery is involved, and because it's only and solely a matter of LIVING: the Woman is there, and some other women.

[09/23/1993] The 23rd.

Salim is back. A long conversation—rather strained—while shelling beans: violence, suffering. God and the religions. "You talk like a fundamentalist.[6] Your references are different. Sometimes I get the impression that you use a language that is not your own . . . ," and then this: "You are tormented." I said: YES, I have every reason to be. I'd love to be able to say it to you because YOU would have become my life. And that would be understood—simply.

[09/25/1993] The 25th.

Yom Kippur.
Taken together in that boundless gesture
taken by mad love
for here one must offer
a response
to the violence of the homicidal lie

6. "Fundamentalist" here translates the French word *intégriste,* a somewhat vague but much-used term applied to persons belonging to contemporary ideological-political movements, often reactionary groupings with a religious foundation.

The other cheek—that's my whole body
lifted up in crucified love
naked vulnerable strong.

You are winning.

[10/02/1993] October 2nd.

Thérèse of the Child Jesus and of the Holy Face has become very close to me. Her written story speaks to me. Her place of stability is the Cross, after her grace at Christmas: "I resolved to stay there continually . . ." She receives LOVE like a fire, a thirst. "I thirst."

A few days ago, a letter from X. "I shall probably never return to Algeria. Never." X. adds: "A pity, yes, it's even a kind of waste." But I see rather a grace that frees: X. untied to live according to the Gospel.

[10/07/1993] October 7th.

Our Lady of the Rosary and the anniversary of my return to this country: to stay here until you come again. It's to that point we (I) must announce your death, announce your surrendered life.

[10/10/1993] The 10th.

Your will on EARTH. Those words from the prayer received from you spoke to me the other day in the vineyard. To realize the WILL of the Father: to exist by reference to Him, in order to do his work here and now.

War (violence) cross toil: everything is here [in Latin in the text: *Ense, cruce, aratro*[7]].

7. Literally, "by the sword, by the cross, by the plough."

[10/20/1993] October 20th.

I am 43 years old. How much longer to hold out here? Yesterday a journalist, 31 years old, was stabbed. Salim has become very close to me. Friendship and intercession: not so much to pray *for* as to feel my prayer pervaded *by* this brother I've received as a friend. I should like to be his shield, his shelter in distress.

I have to win the battle for PEACE within myself. Receive it from your pierced hands.

Today a letter—after some others—from G. in Lebanon. Overflowing and ardent. A passionate child. And all woman.

I had a doubt. About myself. Have I turned an impulse of the heart away from you to me? Perhaps that would be a blasphemy against Love.

Only you can reassure me. Even so, I must keep close to you: in the same place where the Woman and others with Her are with the beloved Disciple, all turned toward you and receiving Communion from you in crucified Love.

[10/23/1993] The 23rd.

I warn you: I am
going through you I go before you and
I breathe into you the Way
and oblige you in truth.
I baptize you with myself on the cross
GO
take my *I love you*
be me

[10/24/1993] The 24th. Sunday.

I warn you
listen well
I am
and look there yes that is where I bleed
for you
touch who you are

Lectio

With this budding day I receive permission for a paschal adventure
Friend what shall we do?
embrace me beloved
and leaving the book I take the opportunity to say
thank you
forgive me
I love you
it is written in your hand
I just have to sign it ✝
(to the child
of the country. Jean Scotto).

[10/24/1993] October 24, 1993.

If a story
should happen to me
one of these days
having to do with BEING BORN
Friend I beg you finish it
and if it pleases you to make me one day
exit from the NIGHT
You my conqueror
FORGIVE ME

do not let go of me
Then
if I succeed
for once
in loving
if I succeed
in being in time
with your heart
and if, in the END, I receive your
I love you ✝

thank you
for kindly HAVING MERCY ON ME.

Rîbat es-Salâm:[8] Watchman, what of the NIGHT?
"Christianity is the great adventure
for through it one is called by an infinite love
that is, by a love that does not cease to ask and to give."

[11/05/1993] Saturday 5th.

At Lauds (Zechariah 12). Father, here we are a people that rises like the dawn with the Woman standing, receiving the Spirit of prayer: to love and adore.

Nourished yesterday by your Mercy piercing me
bond of prayer and of the cross with Denis.
To pray for Henri.

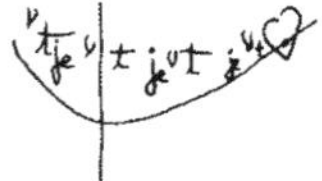

[12/01/1993] December 1st.

Ever since Sunday Mass—it was just at the moment of daring to say Our Father

—these words are working me over and take meaning in my body, in this community-body of which I am part: the ALL-POWERFUL GIFT.

[12/02/1993] December 2nd.

Here there is something to see, to receive, in the night: the Gift that is stronger than death. Mary was the first to be pierced

8. "Bond of Peace," a group that met at Tibhirine engaged in Islamic-Christian dialogue. Father Christian de Chergé was one of its leading lights.

through like Jesus: placed in the axis of that murderous lance that touched her son who was already given over into other hands.

[12/03/1993] December 3rd.

Something in my flesh has taken shape in the form of writing. That is:

The story leads I believe where you know
and I hope the dénouement is near
through the all-powerful Gift.
What must happen soon tears me apart.
And what happens to you here pierces me where
you hold us fast
with arms outstretched.
You ask us to be there
(monks) until the end of the story.
Nothing happens on its own. Everything is but
fulfillment.
And gratitude.
Already Christmas is at the door.
Father, it's about you, in me,
it becomes a question of living according to you: all of us
beloved.
Love one other, says the Child.
For mercy's sake: Let's go forward! Time is short: hurry!
The story expects your Kiss of peace from us.

[12/05/1993] Sunday, December 5th.

At the homily, I heard: "The role of religious in the Church is one of re-collection."

To collect all that is seen, prayed and done here: this calls for a watchful interiority—that of a friend, a friend of the Bridegroom—and then for a tireless opening outward, without fear or selective withdrawal.

The cross is thus made ready where God and man are recollected.

[12/22/1993] Wednesday, December 22nd.

So we had the community retreat with Father Sanson. What has been retained of the points for self-examination? Has there been etched into me something like a definitive, decisive point having to do with prayer? Yes, a point about adoration that You must have put at the end of a phase that I must live and see through to the end without weakening.

The impossible resolution, yes, I have made it: received from You. Love obliges me:

This is my body: given.

This is my blood: poured out.

May it be done unto me according to your word, may your gesture pierce me through.

And this resolution—that is yours: it's infinitely beyond me.

Near the Woman (you, the Son, born of her flesh, give me permission to call her Mama, and to take her to myself), my resolution is very simple: I am.

A resolution stronger than death.

So we had the retreat, concluded on Friday with a heightened awareness: in the situation facing us, how can we hold firm and what should we do? The effort to use our intelligence (Father Sanson's on this occasion) gives a first indication: seek to understand.

It seems to me that there is a "monastic" way of doing it.

Where prayer intervenes and speaks its particular point of view that is indebted to the Spirit and to Scripture.

Saturday morning I was on the road to Fez, accompanied by A. and M. Staying with the four who are in Fez, happy to be "one of them." A peaceful, restful, consoling time: recollection, fraternal life.

Bernard Rérolle's book on the Beatitudes went with me.[9]

9. Bernard Rérolle, French Marist priest who preached the community retreat at Tibhirine in 1996, one month before the abduction. The book in question is *Passage vers l'autre rive : La dynamique des Béatitudes* ("Crossing to the Other Shore: The Dynamics of the Beatitudes," 1987).

"Onward, the humble of breath, the Kingdom of heaven—of God—is theirs."

And what follows: to recognize happiness—a way to conversion.

Father Bernardo,[10] in his conference at the closing of the General Chapter, sends us in that direction.

That ought to be enough to keep me occupied . . . until You come again.

. . . here, suddenly, is my happiness, it's true
my joy: you.

We have been living through various issues here at Tibhirine. Above all: the massacre of the Croats who were working, digging a tunnel, and who lived down there, near us. To hear of it in Fez, and then to live the event that affects us here, is not the same thing.

On my return I find the community deeply marked, affected: deepened in its Christian identity, both human and . . . contemplative.

I must try to integrate in myself what they have lived through.

Like this morning when listening to Ali.

I avoid it too, for it is a question of embracing each brother in his unique way of living his daily life. Reactions of irritation return to me quickly in the face of too many words, or a proud retreat into myself when faced with such a disconcerting and inconvenient attitude. I need to receive the strength to forget myself, at Mary's side—simply: I am.

After Mass.

I am reclaimed by Your resolution: my soul magnifies you. Your resolution is an act of thanksgiving.

Koran II:82: "Those who adhere and are upright are among the Companions in the Garden, they are there forever."

10. Dom Bernardo Olivera, Trappist abbot general during the years when Father Christophe was writing his journal.

86: "Those who barter the Other in exchange for life in this world."

[12/24/1993] The 24th.

Koran II:87: "Thus we gave the Writing to Moussa [Moses] and we let him be followed by other Messengers. We gave the proofs to Issa [Jesus], son of Mariyam [Mary], sustaining him by an inborn breath. But each time a Messenger brought you what your people did not want, you were puffed up, treating some as liars, and killing others."

More intensely, You pray.
Rise up!
Pray so as not to enter the trial.

[12/25/1993] Christmas.

A dark night and the Morning Star lights up every face. We are all alive.

"And the light shines in the darkness, and the darkness has not overpowered it."

It is enough for us to hold on to the power
of becoming children of God
of God begotten here.

[12/26/1993] The 26th.

What has happened to us?
You, who are beyond everything
the Unexpected One revealing our thirst to us: oh come
"See, I come quickly."
Caught in the Event,
we have only to follow the current of grace.
Unbound, in peace,
our eyes have seen.

See what is put in the midst of fragile us like the child
lying in the manger
of us who are vulnerable through and through
like the Lamb,
and ready like the Servant,
see, here is put the SIGN
of contradiction
and we shall be pierced
by the same sword that pierces
your heart
and the heart of Mary
who is our refuge
our conscience
our open shelter
house of prayer
for all.

"Christ, in the face of the Father, is the total surrender of self-will; but, for its realization, the will of the Father relied totally on the initiative of the Son.

"In this surrender the Son is completely free, because he is the gift that has consented absolutely. That is what the Father expects of him, but by himself giving up, through love, all power over his Son.

"The powerlessness chosen by the Father as he made his request means that the submission of his Son will never be domination by the Father. The Son must assume the choice of the gift radically alone, and that is how He carries out the will of the Father. When I ask that the will of the Father be carried out, I strive to give birth in myself to the desire to come face-to-face with the Father, in a relationship analogous to that between the Son and the Father. Only the Spirit can guide me on this way of true life" (Guy Coq[11]).

11. Guy Coq, French Catholic philosopher, disciple of Émmanuel Mounier, author of books such as *La Foi, épreuve de la vie* ["Faith the Test of Life"] and *Inscription chrétienne dans une société sécularisée* ["Christian Insertion in a Secularized Society"].

Human—you, my Lord and my God—human until the end, so that I might today enter into your skin
walk like you as Son
I choose to be loved like you.
You breathe into me this impossible choice.

I look at each one of them—my brothers—whom you have chosen. Christian holds your place: "Monsieur Christian" is the password,
it's the Easter word.

[12/27/1993] The 27th. Saint John, the beloved disciple.

"And our communion is with the FATHER
and with his SON JESUS CHRIST."

You, my little children, who are of GOD, you have conquered those prophets,
because he who is in your midst is greater
than he who is in the world.

"Beloved, if God has loved us so much,
we must have the same love for one another.
No one has ever contemplated God.
If we love one another, God dwells in us, and his love is FULFILLED in us.
In this we RECOGNIZE that we DWELL in him and he in us,
that he has given us his SPIRIT.
And we can WITNESS (because we have CONTEMPLATED him)
that the FATHER has sent his SON
as Savior of the world.
So, to sustain my spirit, I write Scripture: monk-copyist.
I lean on the WORD: In the beginning . . .

[12/28/1993] The 28th.

The Common of Martyrs. Tonight we chanted psalm 32. Verse 11 woke me up.

"The plan of the Lord remains forever,
the designs of his heart hold good from age to age."

And I read what follows with delight: "Happy (onwards!) the people whose Lord You are,"
Beloved Son of the Father, the people in the LOVE that is over us.

Onwards! you poor in spirit.
Yes, you make us run on the way of your commands . . .
not so easy to understand this well.
We are a body that is all ears.

Yesterday H.T. came sent by you to speak to us. He left leaving us free to choose the GIFT in communion with the Church.

Oh, how beautiful she is, Jesus—your resplendent Church.
Oh, keep me close to her
in silence and peace,
a child offered.

[12/29/1993] The 29th.

Mohammed: "As for you, you still have a little door you can escape through.
But we don't: no—no road, no door. This is the best corner of the *wilaya*,[12] of all of Algeria, and they want to . . ."

It's a question of defending far more that a monastery.
"The mission to the people who suffer" opens wide the house of prayer.

Mohammed is like Simeon in the Temple (when he was young!)
this upright and devout man
awaits the CONSOLATION.

12. Arabic administrative unit, in this case a province.

The Church is like the Algerian people: her soul is pierced through by a sword.

[12/30/1993] The 30th.

Anna, the prophetess, adoring night and day
she praises God
and speaks of Him—the Child—
to all those who are awaiting the DELIVERANCE.

Among so many papers to burn, this one attracts my eyes. It says:

"What is desirable is not the excess of the hero who gets drunk on himself, who in his highest exaltation is more closed in on his pride than ever. Desirable is the excess of the saint who, by detaching himself from himself, climbs the highest peaks to the degree that he descends into the deepest humility.

The GOSPEL has no spirit other than this Spirit of holiness communicated by the Crucified in his last breath" (Bernard Ronze, *Faire la vérité* ["To Do the Truth"], p. 101).

The testimony of Jesus, the Christ-like testimony (Alain Chevalier),
is the breath of prophecy.

[12/31/1993] The 31st.

On this day in 1976, the Day of Ashura,[13] Father Jean-Baptiste spoke of offering the twelfth part of fruits and seeds, and then he spoke about YOUR HAND.

And also: about the day of death as the true [monastic] profession.

13. *Ashura:* The Day of Ashura falls on the tenth day of Muharram in the Islamic calendar and marks a very important day of mourning. It is commemorated by Shi'a Muslims as a day of mourning for the martyrdom of Husayn ibn Ali, the grandson of Mohammed.

Into your hands, Mary
into your hands, Church of Algeria
I surrender to crucified Love
that He may profess me
beloved
consecrated in your
I am
Way, Truth, Life.

The Cardinal on the phone yesterday, answering a request for advice from Christian:

persevere in CONSTANCY
you know one must be firm with those people . . . (+ wisdom: rest . . .)

Brother Luc at the Prayer of the Faithful: Lord, give us the grace to die without hatred in our heart.

1994

[01/01/1994] January 1st, 1994. *Mt*

> Mary retains all these things
> and ponders them in her heart.
> This pondering is still going on.

Yesterday, a series of votes at the conventual chapter. And then one finds oneself *alone* again.

I re-read these words that reached us here: "With the help of the holy Spirit, I want to listen to the other and love him. I remain very close to you. You are my beloved brother. While awaiting the joy of seeing you again, I give you a big hug and wish you a good Christmas feast" (Masako, 12/19/93).

Four years ago I was the monk ordained a priest at Tibhirine.

[01/02/1994] January 2, 94 Your Manifestation [Epiphany].

Everything converges toward this place: "Where is the child?"

They come to the house and see the child with Mary, his mother.

The *I am* opens out to us: he draws us.

It's a place to be born in. Close to Mary. *I am.*

They returned by a different way.

And that is what happens, I believe, to each one of us after the shock of the Christmas event. Now we return from there, having undergone conversion almost in spite of ourselves. I myself was led to an extreme, an excessive point. A point of gravity whose weight continues to weigh on my shoulders. I am like everyone here and like our neighbors: tired, weighed down. Indeed, the story of man is a heavy thing. You carry the responsibility for it, you who had nowhere to lay your head, you who go on working unceasingly as you see your Father does. The work of God is the true labor of the monk. I love performing it here. With Mohammed this afternoon; we talked about manure, about plowing . . . W. and Moussa were pruning an apple tree. Ammi Ali came by with his grandson Amin—just to see us with his restless eyes. This place is holy. A place of true adoration in the Breath of the Nazarene. Here, where the little child is, his *I am* as the Beloved is enacted in the body of Mother Church. Will we have to leave? Flee by order of the Most High? For the moment it is a question

of abiding here as in our home,
until YOU come: O LOVE.

[01/04/1994] The 4th.

We are one less already. W. has gone down to Algiers and he will alternate staying there and here at Tibhirine. Paul and Célestin leave tomorrow for Algiers with Christian, and on Thursday for Marseilles. Will endless movement start up again? Will it put an end to this time of recollection?

In the chapel we still have an ALTAR, but smaller, more human-sized.

The crucifix is the one for Lent.

"If you leave you deprive us of your hope, and you take away from us our hope" (Moussa to Christian).

[01/05/1994] The 5th.

"Come along. We're going for our people" (Edith Stein).[1]

Today you tell your terrified disciples to row with the wind against them:

Courage: *I am*. Do not be afraid.

If one understands the Eucharist, one understands everything.

[01/06/1994] The 6th.

Jesus returns in the power of the SPIRIT.
Isn't that what we must do: come back here
in the power of the GIFT
with the STRENGTH of LOVE?
He stands up to READ [in Arabic in the text: *qâma li'yaqra*]
to announce the GOOD NEWS
today . . .

Your joy, yes, that plenitude in my poverty is from you—to be loved like you.

And then, at the office of Lauds, I experience the joy of those who seek shelter in you,

I experience the shield of your favor: it covers us.

M., Ali's son says: "You know, every morning when I go to work, I look at the house to see whether there is LIGHT on. And I say: *hamdulillah* ['praise God!']."

Ben Ali asks: "Is Paul coming back?"

1. These were the words spoken by Saint Edith Stein to her sister Rosa when they were arrested in Holland and were about to be transported to Auschwitz.

[01/08/1994] Saturday, January 8th.

The friend of the bridegroom stands there (stability)
and hears him (listening).

He who moves about and gets agitated cannot listen well—he makes a noise which interferes with your voice.

To listen to you is to be placed where your voice speaks to me: it's the voice of the Bridegroom speaking to the Bride. What you say concerns each one of us

your words of love concern me.
At Mary's side I am in peace and
in a silence that listens.
To listen to you is to receive the place
of stability: to dwell
in your Word
to dwell in your Love
and wait
for You
come quickly
soon
waiting for You here at Tibhirine
waiting: we and the Spirit
oh, Marana tha.

JESUS IS BAPTIZED

He baptizes us in the pure Breath
and sends us into the world, like HIM
loved in the BELOVED
sons in the Son = for all ✝

"Every day we will be

what the love of God makes us to be for each one of our brothers" (Madeleine Delbrêl[2]).

REMAIN HERE and keep watch with ME.

2. Madeleine Delbrêl (1904–1964), French Catholic mystic, social activist, essayist, and poet.

[01/10/1994] Monday in Ordinary Time.

Come after me.

[01/11/1994] Tuesday.

one must be firm with those people,
like you, Jesus, with the demons,
(Mk 1:21-28)
we need your AUTHORITY,
your freedom
we need the Advocate: he will convict
(Jn. 16:8,15) the world
he will take from what is mine and declare it to you
the SPIRIT of truth
he will testify on my behalf
and you also will testify
because you have been with me
from the beginning

The ways of Love are strange:
he who wants to follow them knows this well
[. . .]
One moment humiliated, the next exalted,
hidden now, and then at once exposed
to be overwhelmed one day with sweet love
you must risk many an adventure
before reaching
the point where you taste
the pure essence of Love.

The authority of Jesus in our midst has no trace of violence or arrogance. It does not compete with the forces that are fighting. Its goal is not power, but it cannot make compromises with the homicidal Lie, with idolatrous Money.

The eyes of the poor appeal to your authority in us. Christian said to M., Ali's son: "You know, we are a bit like the bird on the branch." And he answered: "But look: You are the branch. We are the bird. And if they cut off the branch . . ."

There is a Gospel authority here that is recognized as doing more good than the Law: If you were to leave: Tibhirine would finished, there would be nothing but quarrels . . .

We have to draw from the source of your authority, from the love with which you are loved. I must promote your authority in M., "my second-in-command" (!). In each one of those with whom I work. To recognize it and rejoice in it: "I bless you Father for hiding these things . . ."

Good news: there is an authority in this world
stronger than the powerful,
an authority unshaken in the face of the terrorists:
the authority of humility:
of CRUCIFIED TRUTH.

[01/13/1994] January 13th.

In Kabylia, a *wali*[3] and his bodyguards were assassinated; in Algiers, policemen have been killed. At Vigils it was Cain killing Abel. The blood of the just cries out. Your shed BLOOD heals, purifies, vivifies, intercedes.

To intercede, to pray for, is to give the blood of one's heart, says Silouan.[4]

Am I here one who prays? Abel and Cain both prayed.

Jesus, heal me of the violence lurking inside me: the beast. Make me human according to your beatitudes.

You stretch out your hand and touch me: "I want it—Be cleansed." In your BLOOD.

[01/14/1994] January 14th.

Gilles passed through here yesterday (Eucharist together); he brought back W. Coffee that leaves me with a bitter taste I can't get

3. A *wali* is a provincial governor in an Islamic country.

4. Saint Silouan of Mount Athos (1866–1938) was an Eastern Orthodox monk of Russian origin. An ardent ascetic, he received the grace of unceasing prayer and saw Christ in a vision. He prayed and wept for the whole world as for himself, and he put the highest value on love for enemies.

rid of. It's a little as if one wanted to turn the page. Our experience of the season of Advent and Christmas has suddenly been integrated into the "problem" of the Church in Algeria. The important thing is that we haven't left . . . "as I had told (you)." They forgive us for having had the idea. They thank us for being like Moses, interceding on the mountaintop. Bah! Excuse us, father Moses! But you understand: it's all about him in you as well as in us.

What has happened to us is You.

How could we pass on to something else as if there were a next chapter?

At Vigils last night I read the story of the Flood.

And then I read the story of your Passion and Glorification.

You tell Pilate the meaning of this Christmas 1993:

"I was born
and I came into the world
to bear witness to the truth."

Your breath involves us—body and goods—
in your witness,
the witness of Jesus is the breath of prophecy.

Must we make an effort to communicate the fact, to try and make them understand the fact, that this breath has overwhelmed us, traumatized us, as they say . . . and as for me, I'd like not to get too distracted from it, but remain connected to the place where the spirit is breathed out: your Cross.

Here the Way of the Church opens up
here one vows stability as a pilgrim, as one passing through.

[01/15/1994] The 15th.

Where is fidelity? Who obeys? He who says and affirms peremptorily and sure of himself: "I shall never leave this place."

Or another, who says: "I am going to leave," but is still here . . .

persevering in your teaching (GOSPEL here today)
in the monastery until death
(which has come close and still threatens)

taking part in your sufferings, O Christ our Passover
through patience
in order to deserve
to be in your Kingdom
as *partakers*,
eucharisticized
Christified.

In the monastery until death, yes, if and how you want it, but not outside a living faithfulness to your teaching: what the Spirit has said to us during this time of the Church.

But what has the Spirit actually said to us?

It seems to me it has to do with the Church "in the house of Islam." Our neighbors have seen that we were disposed to leave, almost in spite of ourselves. Without quite saying everything—which is useless, because they know much more than we imagine—messages were sent, to the effect that we cannot obey either the *wali* or the guerrillas, but we should like to remain here as monks, men of peace and prayer, and work.

The massacre of the Croats has left us traumatized, for we are not armor-plated by our enclosure. It defines a space of welcome and has the form of an open heart: wounded by the suffering of this world, it offers a resolution of crucified Love in the face of the enemy.

Our conviction that we had to leave the monastery expressed a solidarity that was revived by the events of December 24 and emphasized by Christian. Has our Christian community denounced this massacre?

This radical suspicion torments me: we
monks
psychotics
artisans of idiocy
they say: pray for us
and let us make the decisions
you are incapable of.

I believe in Gilles's friendship. But I don't ignore my limits as a monk in the process of conversion.

Is he yet another guest of God
he whose guests have been slaughtered
he on whom one imposes particular conditions "of
hospitality."
Wouldn't it be doing a favor to our Muslim friends
to clarify what has happened . . .
not without risk to us and them?

[01/16/1994] Sunday.

During the night I performed an infinite service on your behalf by saying: I forgive you.

Do I know my body as being for You and You for my body?

I cannot say whether I am UNITED to you, I simply weep and beg that I may never be separated from You,

temple of the Breath that is in me
coming from the Father, given by you,

and I do not belong to myself: Mary is the guarantor in me of that detachment that was total and radical in her.

Close to her: I am. Then I will be able to glorify You through my body.

In a long conversation this morning, Christian talked to me about his refusal to imagine that his death could possibly be imputed to those whom he loves here. He recalled Brother Luc's prayer during Mass: "Lord, let me be able to die without hatred in my heart," and also Geneviève B., steeping herself in Jesus' words: "No one takes my life from me, I lay it down of my own free will." And Gilles: three minutes to say YES.

I then spoke about what had happened on the evening of the 24th: which was lived as a flight, then a waiting, then an ascent from the abyss.

Where have you led me? For me, perhaps it means accepting to live. But can you ask me to accept the death of my brothers?

Two events are tied together in my memory today. Granma ill with cancer, and a call within me: to take her place so that she may live. What does this mean here, today, without imagining anything? What meaning for my life?

"I have faith in obedience."

Christian said: "Joseph also obeyed Jesus with Mary."

[01/17/1994] Saint Anthony.

"The wedding guests," the Gospel says today. Yes, that's what we are here.

You are here. You are not here. You ask us to be here as witnesses to your indissoluble marriage as God and man. No question of fasting when you are in our midst, saying: "Take, eat, drink. My Body. My Blood. For you and for all."

And in 1 Samuel: obedience is better (than sacrifices)
docility is more (than the fat of rams)

Yesterday, I read the Christmas greetings from our cardinal: "Keep your trust in the Church high."

And then I come across these words in a note (that escaped the fire) from Father Denis, dated March 24, 1991:

> "Yes, God is magnificent in Love, in Mercy toward his children, he is only waiting for the gift of our heart to invade it, to fill it to overflowing with himself: Complete happiness . . . that we may in turn give it away to others for his joy."

Last night, Father P. Sandrin (deceased) came to visit me in a dream. He spoke to me.

[01/18/1994] Tuesday.

- The act of transmitting his Breath (Jn 19:30) to a group whose salient feature is its approach to the cross in an attitude of faith, and independently of all other claims: this is directly in line with the Johannine project. (Alain Chevalier)
- V. 23 (Jn 20) announces that, following the Son and inspired by his breath, there will appear a ministry of pardon and condemnation in the world, a ministry of judgment *(krisis)*. In the Johannine perspective, the whole community continues the course of the Son in the world. (A. Chevalier)

- To live according to the Eucharist means literally to tear oneself loose from one's own narrow, particular life in order to grow toward the immensity of the life of Christ. Whoever has visited the Lord in his dwelling will no longer be uniquely concerned about himself and his own interests: he begins to take an interest in the affairs of the Lord. (Edith Stein)

In solitude in the novitiate. I receive a promise from you:
whoever drinks the water that I shall give him
will never be thirsty for all eternity
but the water that I shall give him will become in him
a source of water spring up into eternal life.
I read Silouan.
Please Jesus: your Humility
please my Beloved: your Love, your power to FORGIVE.

[01/19/1994] The 19th.

Today: David's battle against Goliath.
He puts aside breastplate, sword and shield
here it's good for us to be "lightly" armed
he takes his staff in hand
we simply need to hold the cross
the staff of victory
for it's not by sword or javelin that You give victory
You, you are the master of the battle
when the powerful, the violent,
when the liars cry the opposite
and would have us believe it, imposing
their conditions on us one by one.
No, You are the master of the battle, You impose on us the rules of crucified Love.
You deliver our enemies
into our open praying hands.

You entrust Forgiveness to us, in the power of your Breath of truth
in order to insert it here into the history of Algeria

in order to inscribe it as our Christ-like contribution
to its recovery.

Stand up in the middle of the assembly
stretch out your hand.

This morning Kader comes running on his way home from school. He sees his father plowing the field where I was spreading manure with a pitchfork. "Baba! Baba!" "Kadi."

I feel a little pang at not being greeted like this and at not being Baba. And then I become aware of my childlike happiness. I can say to Him and I do say it: "Baba! Baba!"

To Him who works always, and I too . . . work!

Beginning the Eucharist, Christian stresses Saul's reaction to David: "You're only a child!"

And at stake there's the struggle of the Child.

[01/20/1994] The 20th.

Give me a drink: of you. My mouth wide open, I breathe in.

What you say to me (to us) is: breath and life.

I receive the mission to be a wellspring: it's You in me, leaping up into eternal Life.

A mission to breathe.

[01/21/1994] Friday.

In our Church: prayer and fasting for PEACE, particularly in the former Yugoslavia.

Father, I pray for those who, thanks to their word, believe in me.

[01/22/1993] And Saturday.

Forty days ago: the massacre of our Croatian brothers at Tamesguida.

[01/23/1994] The 23rd.

Presided and gave the homily at Mass on this day of the Lord: with the happiness of a child.

It's not always like that. Sometimes it demands a lot and is hard to get through.

I read Éloi Leclerc:[5] *Rencontre d'immensités* ["Encounter of Immensities"]. I'm right there with Pascal through my unique experience that now always refers me back to the *I love you* I heard in my little room when I was a student in Tours, and also to those two hours of Vigils on Christmas Eve, 1993. "Jesus in agony until the end of time": we mustn't sleep. Father, if it is possible . . . Jesus uncertain about the will of the Father. Death, F.L. writes, is not programmed. It is not evident that it is willed by God. Jesus came to announce the joyful news of the Kingdom.

This afternoon, Brother Luc tells me that a Tunisian Jew has been murdered. That death cannot have been programmed. Jesus gives it meaning through his free commitment as crucified Love.

[01/24/1994] January 24, 94.

Dreams: the other night I was asking about Jean-Bernard. There were quite a few (handicapped) people in the room, but he wasn't there. No possibility of meeting. Last night Ali, some others and myself tracked down a mad boar. It was wounded and chased us. Wild flight. . . . And at Vigils it's Lot's turn to flee: "Run for your life." Earlier he had denounced Evil. When threatened, he was saved by a hand. The hand made him go into the house, then made him go out again. This may clarify our situation. What matters is: not to let go of your HAND. You are stronger than the strong.

5. Éloi Leclerc (b. 1921), French Franciscan, poet, philosopher, and concentration camp survivor of World War II.

[01/25/1994] Conversion of Saint Paul.

This Gospel is not inspired by humans. God has called me by his tender love to discover him in myself so that I may proclaim him. No one comes to the Son except by the Father's Gift. No one conceives the Son but the Father. Only the Spirit fathoms the Relationship.

To discover you in me, Jesus, Son of the Father, is also to recognize myself as a marvel in the eyes of Mercy. "Come and see: he told me everything about me."

The mission, before all preaching, is to listen to the Son, to receive your Gospel in me. The Church is first of all an evangelized body. And the house of your breath of truth: it is flesh and blood, not an abstract construction or a theoretical scaffolding.

When the disciple whom you love hears: here is your
mother,
this is a Revelation in me
of your *I*.

[01/26/1994] The 26th.

The New Monastery.[6]

Return to the Gospel as pure source through the Rule of Saint Benedict.

I read chapter 72. What I lack: to love with true love. To love like you.

Last night at Vigils I heard Christian proclaim (from Mark 10): "Children, how difficult it is to enter into the Kingdom of God."

You must make us enter. Make me enter, I beg you. Remember . . .

I heard Peter: we have dropped everything, left everything behind.

6. "New Monastery" was the original name given to the new Benedictine foundation at Cîteaux in 1098. The founding of the Cistercian Order is celebrated on January 26, "Founders' Day," the feast of Saints Robert, Alberic, and Stephen.

And I heard you, Jesus: for my sake and for the Gospel.

"You shall receive." We receive here, according to the measure of our detachment. And persecutions besides?

[01/27/1994] The 27th.

It was in Fez that I felt in my whole being a desire to unwind, to rest.

To satisfy that desire, what do you offer me?

Must I go looking elsewhere: outside the enclosure . . . outside the vows of religion?

Must I go scatter myself, let off steam? Go and forget this burning that demands so much?

In Fez, I heard a somewhat updated version of your Beatitudes. "Happy!" now becomes "Onward!" But ever since then . . . , I am even thirstier. A thirst for tenderness, too. Last night at Vigils, the servant beside the well received water from the hands of beautiful Rebecca.

> "The water that I myself will give him."
>
> Mary in me: draw the inaccessible water and give me some of it, I beg you. I thirst for Him.
>
> Mary near the Wellspring in me.

I love to see M. engaged in his work, tilling his own land of Algeria.

> "Blessed are the meek, for they will possess the land": as an inheritance from you. The people are so far from being able to take possession of their heritage. . . . May we in our very small measure help them to get their rights, contribute to this blessedness and its demands.

[01/28/1994] Friday.

Reading the story of your Passion according to Mark, then Isaiah 53.

Who will tell its story? Who will speak of the massacre of those men of sorrows—Croatians without beauty or importance?

Christian's letter to *La Croix*[7] involves us in an ongoing story that is forever happening to us and will unfolding until the End.

He will see the fruit of his labor.
Yes, this labor of faith allows us to SEE
and have our fill.

Michel yesterday morning. As he was mopping the floor he stopped, looked up at me with his very limpid gaze and let out, without barely opening his mouth: "It's no longer like before. Ever since they came, I've no more strength."[8]

I've thought about what I wrote in this journal: this thirst for happiness. Oh, if I could only tap into the immense reservoir of happiness, this available joy that consists in giving, in loving Michel, and Paul who came back yesterday, and Célestin who is away, being tried, and each one of them: loved by You, with a crucified love. Resolution.

Mission: the true story of crucified Love. "You will do this in memory of me."
"Whom are you looking for?" *I am.*

[01/30/1994] Sunday.

Jesus at Capernaum teaches with (prophetic) authority. In December 1990 I was there, walking into the very space where your voice struck them with amazement.

And I know today that if I leave this listening space, I am lost. I die.

Your authority as a free man is felt among us who are so weak, who are so little, and really nothing, without you. You impose silence on the Liar. Come quickly to my heart, so menaced by darkness. Teach me to know and recognize the special tone of your authority hidden in each one of my brothers, in every

7. French Catholic daily paper.
8. This probably refers to the guerrilla's first threatening "visit" to the monastery.

human being. I do not yet love your freedom in the other: a marvel. Let me begin by loving myself in your freedom.

"To prophesy is to speak of God, not through proofs from the outside, but through interior and immediate feeling." (Pascal, *Pensées*, 328)

Do we not have this Spirit of prophecy over our community?

Brother Luc just spoke to us in chapter, before joining the "Octogenarians' Club" tomorrow. "Tibhirine has *resisted* the war, resisted the terrorists . . . and that's mysterious. At my moment of death, if it's not violent, I ask you to read to me the parable of the Prodigal Son and that to say the JESUS prayer.[9] And then, if there is any, give me a glass of champagne to say goodbye to this world . . . before tasting the NEW WINE."

I cut out an article from *La Croix*. In it Christian Bobin[10] writes: "Today, military solutions seem to be taking over. So what can we do about it? We must resist, resist."

"To resist evil is to resist the world, and to resist the world is to act politically when the politicians no longer are doing it. [. . .] It is not a question of being optimistic, but rather of not giving in to the gloomy spirit of this gloomy world. It means leaning on the only strength in ourselves that is inexhaustible, the strength of the child. No empire, no matter how powerful, can perdure before the incredible weakness of childhood, before the truth of this weakness. [. . .] Passing from the spirit of this world to the spirit of childhood engages all our being and renews everything."

I was just listening to Dvořák, tears running down my face: the *Slavonic dances*. They invited me to join in.

[02/01/1994] February 1st.

"Absalom, Absalom, my son, my son," David exclaims, his heart pierced. Joab reproaches him: you love those who hate you.

9. Also known as "Prayer of the Heart," an Eastern Christian custom that repeats the Name of Jesus as often as possible during the day.

10. Christian Bobin (b. 1951), French Catholic writer.

"But I say to you: love your enemies." Onward we go, those whose wombs are compassionate!

Lord, I am heavy. Give me your vitality. To the far end of Faith.

Make me into a spring flowing from YOUR HEART.

Reorganization of the choir. The goal is recollection, to foster listening in communion. I am opposite you—the Crucified One who draws me into your LIFE. The altar binds us together. I sorely need your Breath as a friend, to make an act of faith, an act of singing—may it never lift itself above the breath proper to a servant. May this not displease the liturgists.

Your joy left behind
like a guest to be welcomed,
keeping the right tone and the pace
of humility: You.

[02/02/1994] 2/2, death of Father Pierre.

Last images of my dream just as the bell interrupted it (it's a simple one): a small child (Amin, Robah's son; met them yesterday when I was coming back from the vineyard), hit (crushed?) by a car that was backing up. A cry.

The reading at Vigils yesterday made sense of the enclosure, of the monastery as the house of God. At Bethel, Jacob receives this place from on high: the place of the Presence. And because there is an exchange, it is a place of offering, since that is how one has access to the heights. A House that is a Gate. Jacob continues on his way.

We are the house. Our discussions and the votes of the community at Christmas have clearly manifested this *we* as something living, surviving. Our ultimate vocation is not the defense of a temple. We have experienced being your body
pierced by a sword
indwelt by your Breath
it is He who defends our Christ-identity.

Yesterday I was told of an event in the ongoing story: Robert's house has been looted, turned into ruins, for being the home of a Christian.

By the military?

"Now you can let your servant go in PEACE."

My eyes see you, JESUS: a sign of contradiction: The Child

so that the sign may continue

here is your son
here is your mother.

The sword that pierces the heart of the Church
is the death of her children
here joy is pointing
to the ultimate Hope.

"A mad prayer," writes Little Sister Marie-Danièle

I pray madly, a little too much so,
not at all
"excuse me, please, make me . . ."
a mad prayer
of crucified
Love.

[02/03/1994] Thursday.

Dreaming last night: on a station platform.

Two trains are about to depart. I hesitate and take the second. It's going to Tours but doesn't pass through Blois.

One February 2nd, at Tamié,[11] I took the train to Tours where Dad was in the hospital.

In the Gospel (Mk 6) today, you call to Yourself and then you send out. The sending out is detachment, tearing apart, adventure. Here, You give us authority: your freedom in us. It's this freedom that rids us of everything useless that so slows down Christian swiftness, burdens it and weighs it down.

11. Monastery of Trappist monks in the French Alps, the original monastery Brother Christophe Lebreton entered.

Take nothing for the journey.

The closure of a mission: if some place does not receive you, stay there until you can get out.

[02/04/1994] Friday.

Reading of the story of your PASSION. We are there, through patience (that I sorely lack).

You say: now, my royalty is not from here. This "now" moves me to tears: giving, forgiving. Mercy from age to age: without which history would stop, paralyzed by so many crimes and lies.

You say—to Her: "Woman, this is your son." I believe in such a birth certificate

And to me: "This is your mother." Taking her to my home opens me to her labor of giving birth: patience.

It is your Day. Please, make it rise in my night. As for you, in the Gospel (Mk 1:29-39) you get up in the middle of the night, go out and leave for a lonely place. There, time and again you pray. *There:* it is up to us to give body to that place. To be your body here at prayer at night. Turned toward the Father and available to go to that Elsewhere to which you are sent. A prayer of infinite opening: so that all may LIVE. A prayer that embraces the burning demand: that receives the Gospel to tell it, to shout it. That is what you went out for.

May we not fail to encounter that Elsewhere here and now.

Night is—I said this to myself during Eucharist—when one no longer sees one's own image clearly. I surrender my whole being to YOU.

A monk is a nocturnal creature. How could I achieve intercession, vicarious representation of others and supplication, if I do not stop worrying about myself? In the darkness of the cellar, this past December 24, you began to teach me this lesson, when I thought that the others were in the hands of the "visitors" . . .

In the refectory at noon today we hear read *Les hommes de la fraternité* ["The Men of the Brotherhood"], pp. 58–59: "We must strip down to the essentials this idea of supplication, this image of suppliants, we must purify it of all platitudes. [. . .] In ancient tragedy, it is not the one who is being entreated but rather the suppliant who at bottom has the upper hand in the supplication, the upper hand in the dialogue. [. . .] The suppliant represents. He is no longer only himself. He is no longer himself. It is no longer a question of him. [. . .] It is he, the suppliant, the man bowed down at the feet of the other, who dominates the supplication, the operation, the business of the supplication; he is the master, and he speaks an elevated language, a master language coming from afar, coming altogether from elsewhere." (Charles Péguy,[12] *Cahiers de la quinzaine*)

The language of the one who prays the Psalms. Samuel the Suppliant. And on the cross, God is entreating: crucified Love.

A letter from Father Bernardo. Rome, January 21st: "It is still impossible to foresee how events will evolve now, but in your way of living the grace 'of the present moment' you may be certain that the Lord is with you, fulfilling his promise: 'I shall be with you always, until the end of the world'; for 'where two or three are gathered together in my name, there I am in the midst of them.' And as I said in the homily at the beginning of the General Chapter, he is with you ready to make use of unforeseen means to overcome all obstacles and act with the grace of salvation in this history that is yours . . . and ours."

[02/08/1994] Tuesday.

We are a people that bears the Name: our identity comes from saying "Our Father." The Cross: breathing in and breathing out in the surrendered Breath are one and the same thing. Absence in me of joy, of charity. Not to despair. With the survivors of Sarajevo, with the multitude of those humiliated, to be held

12. Charles Péguy (1873–1914), noted French poet, essayist, and editor who became a fervent Catholic. The *Cahiers de la quinzaine* was a literary and philosophical journal he launched.

between your hands means to be held to supplication: Quickly Our Father, deliver me, deliver us from EVIL.

Mk 7:1-13: They keep the tradition *(sunna)* of the ancients. If it were a question for the Church here, today, of keeping, holding on to, a human tradition, it would be a compromised mission and a loss of energy. It's God's tradition that *holds us.* We hold on to what Jesus has told us to do. And bowing his head, he gives up his Breath. Thus does the Son continue to be handed over: for the salvation of all.

[02/09/1994] Wednesday.

The trap of an obedience that is too smooth and gentle. It flew into pieces two days ago in a discussion about the kitchen sink. Proud self-affirmation of a despicable ego? Or survival instinct? I'm crushed because I hurt someone else. Without strength to move forward. And I hear You saying to me today: it's what comes from within that defiles you.

Deep within and truer than the ego: *I am*. I become pure by placing my hope in You—the only Pure One.

[02/10/1994] Thursday.

Célestin is in the hospital.

Jesus (Mk 7:24-30) at the frontier. Because of this gospel word, you too must go there.

This morning I spoke up myself, and before you I asked for the healing of my rebel heart: that of the child who had an unclean spirit. Now I abide in peace and silence: a child of God—that is what I am. Before Lauds I read something by Jean-Claude Sagne:[13] "The sacrament of reconciliation brings a particular peace, which is to restore the priority of the love of God. The love of God is stronger than all else, stronger than sin and death, stronger also than all brokenness and fear. God's forgiveness is

13. Jean-Claude Sagne, OP (1936–2010), French Dominican priest and social psychologist.

the sovereign intervention of the creative love that can cure beyond what we dare imagine or ask for. The liberating influence of the love of God in our lives may, in addition, provoke the most genuine healing, which is the simplicity of the child's adherence to the desires of its Father.

"Deepening our prayer to Mary makes us tend toward such essential simplicity.

"Union with Mary's surrender and adoration before the will of the Father results in our being drawn into the movement of Jesus' total self-offering, which gives birth to the Church and launches her mission." (*Traité de théologie spirituelle* ["Treatise of Spiritual Theology"], p. 167)

And it's you, Mary, that I saw yesterday as I listened to Jean-Pierre reading to us in the refectory. In an article titled "The Art of Remaining Standing," Milena Jesenská revealed the secret of it with precision: "It is the very essence of anguish not to be able to remain firmly in place. [. . .] By simply remaining standing, I face calmly what I do not know, and I prepare to confront this unknown. [. . .] But to be able to do that, one needs strength; and the individual has only got this strength as long as he does not separate his own destiny from that of others, as long as he does not lose sight of the essential and retains a deep awareness of belonging to a community."

Indeed, and when Peter said: "I'm not one of them," he lost that strength and became a traitor, while Mary—with the other women and the beloved disciple—remained standing.

[02/11/1994] Friday.

How could we intervene effectively in this conflict between brothers?

Like a child ✝ already praying.

The Church as a sign: of your Kingdom now, not from here.

The rest is a matter of listening, of obedience.

Ramadan has begun. Christian is in Morocco. I now have to play a role: in truth. Will I be well inspired? Breathe into me!

[02/12/1994] Saturday 12th.

What a joy to meet Mohammed, Ali or Moussa. In them, the Mystery flowers with simplicity and purity. It's a quality of presence: peaceful, tender, nourishing.

[02/13/1994] Today: Your Day. The 13th here. You say: I will it. Be pure.

[02/15/1994] Tuesday 15th.

Don't you understand? What must be understood, the only thing to know is: the GIFT.

Father Bernardo writes to us: "To receive means to welcome, not only to welcome others but also oneself being welcomed. The Eucharistic prayer is a communion in mutual self-surrender and mutual welcome. That way the word of the Lord is fulfilled: 'You in me and I in you'" (Jn 14:20).

[02/17/1994] Thursday. Lent 1994. It's started.

From the community discussion Monday night, I recall this: "To be attentive to the needs of the people, to what they are living." But from Father Amédée I heard: Compassion and . . . good humor. And these words that launch my Lenten reading (*Treatise of Spiritual Theology*, by J.-C. Sagne): The SECRET OF THE HEART, it seems to me, is: "I and my Father are ONE."

[02/18/1994] Friday.

Jesus is the one who has never withdrawn from anyone bearing his own flesh, because you have never withdrawn from the Love of the Father, no matter how baffling it may be.

A friendly visit by Mohammed and Bashir. Mohammed says: "Algerians have become poor, very poor. They are alone. They have no one to turn to. The Algerian people has been destroyed.

They no longer 'react.'" And he notes the difference between Algerians and the Breton fishermen he's seen demonstrating on TV. The children? Traumatized. "My granddaughter, who's 12 or 13, has asked me for a veil . . ."

Jesus, you say: *I am.* Without evasion, without lying.

Prayer is extreme attention to others, to those of the same flesh. Even in the case of enemies. Prayer is the just, the free attitude. Mary praying: the Eucharistic Church, receiving Love from Jesus with a view: to everybody.

Gilles is with us for Eucharist. After the wash-up we gather around him for an informational "chapter" about the Church (Priests' Council) and about the country. The future is bleak. In the afternoon we hear of the assassination last night of one or two policemen, and of the plunder of shops in Medea.

[02/19/1994] And Saturday.

In Medea, again the other night, they did their deadly work, they have intensified the gloom. But there is this special time opened to us, to me, the Night of your BIRTH. And they said: until EASTER. We cannot envisage anything further away than that. It is a time of renewal, flowing from the Source. But between now and then, I have a radical conversion to accomplish: to become a little child. Because I was born anew last December 24th: you drew me from the pit and made me climb up from the abyss. In order to LIVE: through you, with you, for YOU and in YOU toward the Father.

The secret. It appeals to a childlike heart: without it, it could not risk intimate trust, complicity, sharing of secrets. The meeting point of such mutual trust is the table that is open to sinners, to little dogs, to prostitutes, to children. It's the table of the ultimate secret: "This is my body, this is my blood."

This secret makes appeal to my body: to take it as an offering. At this price it can expand, hand itself over: the secret of your *I love you* for the multitude.

[02/20/1994] And the First Sunday of this Lent, 1994.

The secret of the desert: "I and my Father are ONE." The secret of the Love that has conquered Evil. Forty days to learn your secret by heart, Jesus. GOD's secret: the Gospel of his heart. The really big conversion—"Be converted and believe the Good News"—which means: "unless you change and become like these little children . . .": a radical poverty that is assent to what I am, and an opening in faith to mad Love, to the crucified Love that loves me like this.

To see the rainbow that binds together the heart of my brother, of every human being, of every thing, to the wounded heart of the Spouse (in dialectical Arabic, the word "espoused" is contained in the expression "rainbow" [in Arabic in the text: *'ars al-samâ'*]).

Célestin has had a heart operation in Nantes. How wide it is, our small community of Tibhirine-Fez. The enclosure of the Cross: the strictest one when it comes to openness.

[02/21/1994] And Monday.

Your heart enjoys continuity of ideas—those of the Father— . . . and thus you make us live here today. The sky is blue, the color of a marriage covenant.

And so . . . you give me three words for this Lent: prayer, good humor, and compassion. You give your servant the task of putting them into a sentence with no effort or concern for stylistic elegance. It must only be an authentic sentence about your story here, the story of your *I love you.*

[02/22/1994] Tuesday.

Last night, dreams: a friendly visit from Jean Denis, and then a nightmare that left me paralyzed, nailed to my bed: the big paw of an animal (a bear?) resting on me. The Animal—not in my dream—continues its work of death: at the market in Medea yesterday morning, they found the head of a youngster—a mere boy, Mohammed tells me—and in Algiers last night: a French bookseller murdered.

To ask for that "gift of the Father that binds us tenderly to [the poor, to all those who are 'broken beings' through my lack of humanity], by means of the Body and Blood of his Son" (Father Bernardo Olivera).

[02/25/1994] Friday.

Christian has been here since yesterday; he came back by the power of the GIFT. I step back into the ranks. However, there is no question of melting into a collective, but of being ONE—alone in trust—among others. Singularity does not feel the need of making itself noticed, something that usually can only be achieved at the detriment, or disadvantage, or simply the inconvenience of somebody or other, . . . actually of everybody. Singularity depends on You, the Unique One.

An overwhelming letter. I must read it again. Words of infinite communion. A little cross came with the letter from M.E. The audacity of offering this Tau for Brother Mine, or even better . . . His Oder (?).[14] Such is life! I have put this gift that belongs to You, Brother, as First among us, on the Icon, so that it will become steeped in You: Body and Blood on the wood.

Now that I have read the story into which your Passion invites me, I am going to take my cross, a childlike gift. And I shall ask Mary, blessed among women, to put it around my neck.

Beloved, may she keep me close to you, and transfigure me into a SIMPLE BROTHER here, until I am conformed to the GIFT's excess.

And I copy these words from my Lenten reading that touched me just now in the scriptorium. By Thérèse Couderc:[15] "To hand oneself over is more than devoting oneself, it is more than giving oneself, it is even more than abandoning oneself to

14. Lacking more context, the translator is hard put to decipher this sentence fragment. The original reads: *Audace d'offrir ce Tau pour Frère Mien, mieux encore . . . Son Oder (?).*

15. Thérèse Couderc (1805–1885), foundress of the Congregation of the Sisters of the Cenacle.

God. To hand oneself over is, at bottom, to die to everything, and no longer to concern oneself about the self, except to keep it turned to God always.

"To hand oneself over, furthermore, is never to seek oneself in anything, either spiritual or material, that is, no longer to seek one's own satisfaction but only God's good pleasure. It should be added that to hand oneself over is also that spirit of detachment that holds on to nothing, neither persons nor things nor time nor places. It means to adhere to everything, to accept everything, to submit to everything."

[02/26/1994] Saturday.

How did I dare to write those things yesterday! It was very rash! Or rather, it was to involve myself a little more in the Meaning. The saints did it resolutely, and in communion with them one may receive something singular from them that expressed the Meaning of the Cross at a certain time, in a certain place, through one body, in one history. It seems to me that this Tau on my chest makes me a little bit Franciscan (and Poor Clare!). Oh, to become poor, a true *poverello*. And Donatella finishes her letter in Italian!

[02/27/1994] Second Sunday of Lent.

Instead of speaking from inside the Gospel—which is what Mary does by keeping silence—I say a few words on the margin. Afterwards I ask myself what it can possibly mean to rise from the dead. What experience of transfiguration are we having here on this mountain? A beautiful light is cast on obedience by the first two readings. Abraham, says the text (Gen 22), did not refuse, and then the Lord declares: Since you have obeyed me. . . . Thus, obedience is just that: not to refuse. I think of Célestin, who did not refuse in the end: an obedient brother. And then Saint Paul says of God, in the Letter to the Romans, that He is for us: "He did not refuse [to give] his own Son." The Father obeys the Son: in Him, it is we whom He obeys: by giving us everything.

Obedience must be mutual if it is to be according to God's own pattern. An obedience that binds one to the other in the Gift that obliges us. Let us listen, says Benedict, with eyes wide open, to the voice of the Beloved. Crushed and humiliated, my Servant will see the LIGHT. Transfiguration.

"The fear of being nothing," D. writes to me, "(this is not humility) and the fear that my life may lack all meaning. Yes, but each time there is the same luminous voice that keeps me from falling. The voice that once made Mary turn away from the empty tomb. Maybe all my suffering and despair is necessary for me fully to experience that it is He who saves me, He who loves me, He who desires my joy . . . , that I may share it.

"I often think of Jesus' cry on the cross: 'My God, my God, why have you forsaken me?' In Him, who has experienced solitude and abandonment, I find the ally of all my battles.

"One day the face of the suffering Servant took up his 'abode' in my heart and I cannot erase the fact.

"I have sensed that Christian is shaped by the Word, and this has given me hope for all of you."

A card is enclosed: Mary in labor pains.

I love to re-read the letter from Solange Paule, reminding me of her retreat with her sisters here last summer. You do remember, don't you, the flight into Egypt? You suggested this to us: "Maybe that is what spiritual childhood consists in, and then also to leave a place, a home, for an exodus. . . . I hope that we shall do an in-depth re-reading of this great passing from one place to the other . . . and ask whether that has permitted an Encounter with the Presence in our inmost self.

"Yes, it's in that reality that I have touched his Presence, and together with Him I can make an oblation. I was touched by Christian's trust. . . . Your friend Etty."[16] "Suddenly death is there, great and simple and maternal, having entered my life

16. "Etty": Esther Hillesum, Dutch Jewish diarist (1914–1943), famous for her diaries written 1941–1943 about life in Holland during the Nazi occupation. These diaries were published posthumously under the title *An Interrupted Life*.

without a sound. From now on it has its place there and I know it is inseparable from life."

I am also touched when I re-read the words that Monique de Chergé, Christian's mother, wrote on the letterhead: "The flowers of the field do not move about to seek the rays of the sun: God takes care to make them fruitful where they are."

"Wisdom, Prudence and Trust . . . I am more at Our Lady of Atlas than here. I place my petitions in the hands of the Blessed Virgin. . . . I remain very close to you in heart and prayer."

And also from Dad and Mom, accepting the distance and communing in the Gift that binds us, in the good will of the One who loves us. And: Nadia.

Alone (cenobites in the desert) with you who are seizing us: here, on this mountain.

[03/01/1994] Tuesday, March 1st.

Day after day one must continue to take the blows of the Adversary. In the mosque at Hebron the enemy has plundered everything; he has roared in an assembly of Maronites in Lebanon; and all around us here the dwelling of your name—living man—has been profaned. Heads are cut off, throats are slit. Mohammed M. said last night: "Behind all this there is a force that wants to divide, to turn believers against one another."

We must pray. In Jerusalem, in Lebanon, in Algeria, in Sarajevo. . . . It's dangerous everywhere. The one who prays is vulnerable, disarmed.

The prayer of the child: your cross invites us to that. It draws me to itself . . . in Tibhirine. The prayer of one who has no other defense but you: sustained by your Breath.

Christian speaks to us at Terce: he relates to one another the alms of the Spirit (he is the alms between the Father and the Son . . .); the prayer of the Son (he is Prayer); the fasting of the Father in his dispossession, in his "lack," which is eternally being filled, surfeited by Jesus, the Bread of eternity. Each of the three pillars thus presented has its own personality in this interplay of relationships.

Letter from Philippe: the friend who is my brother. And deacon, until proof of a greater love.

[03/02/1994] Wednesday.

At Vigils, Michel reads the desert saying of the elder who entrusts his garden to a brother. "My friend," he says to himself, "since you have some free time, look after the garden." And the brother stands all day reciting psalms and praying with tears. Then, returning to the elder, he says: "God will provide for the fruits of our little garden."

Today, in the gospel, you take us with you: you say to us on the road . . . [in Arabic in the text: *fi al-tarîq*]. You say: "we" will go up. And all the rest happens to us, too: *we* are betrayed, condemned, scoffed at, scourged and put on the ✝, and on the third day we rise up after being awakened. What happens to us is beyond us: it is you who here give us your cup to drink. All the rest to come at the end of the road—all that must be entrusted by us over and over each day along with you into the hands of the Father, who is always greater. The resolution of crucified Love is exactly as Christian interpreted it. The resolution of self-entrusting Love. It means acting on what I resolve when you give me your Body and your Blood. It means being free: resolved to receive the Gift.

Brother Luc tells me he's indignant, "revolted" by the horrible crime committed in Algiers against a "15-year-old girl," found guilty of not wearing the *hijab* as she walked alongside her friend who was wearing one. Hands chopped off at the market in Medea.

This afternoon: Amin, four years old (as he tells me), stayed alone with me in the garden a good while because his grandfather Ali forgot him. We toiled at your Work. It makes me feel much younger to hear him say "my brother."

[03/04/1994] Friday.

You speak to me—when I say and sing: "I, through the greatness of your love, have access to your house."

There you are in me—so distant yet so close:
In You I have access to my self, delivered to the love
with which You're loved, if anyone loves me—
and how can I say *I love you* if not thanks to your
own Breath
we shall come to him
I and my Father.

Before leaving to go and see Célestin, Christian shares an impression that's remained with him from the night of December 24th to the 25th. Once he had asked the "visitors" to lay down their weapons, he felt great strength in speaking man to man, yes, he felt the strength of the Word and its crucified Truth.

Yesterday R. came for breakfast [*ftur* in the text]. A promising slip of the tongue: he called me Christian. But what spoiled it for me this morning was the talk he gave us in chapter. There was a very moralizing tone to his words, singing the praises of serenity, with it all boiling down to: "Don't be melodramatic." This was aimed at the bishop, at Christians, at us, at me. I said I couldn't bear it. I am sick of it. Opposition touches a certain way of understanding you, Jesus Christ. He seemed so sure of himself and of the rightness of his idea. He seemed to me more intelligent than you. In the end, what can be said? It seems the whole thing is endorsed by the Cardinal.

You—your concern, your anguish, your agony—is all about us. It's about not losing anyone except Judas. Judas precisely.

And I heard your "one must" as sweeping away all opposition, even if it came from a brother in the faith. I heard you were supposed to have said: "I go up." But on a card that Christian sent Célestin yesterday I read: "Behold, *we* are going up."

Mt 20:18: You say "we" in order to include us in the drama of what happened afterwards, for it concerns you and the others, who are involved in what happens to you as you are handed over, condemned, scoffed at, tortured, hung on the cross. The dénouement is not dramatic. I haven't given it sufficient attention: you waking up. The meaning is only there: Resurrection. But from here to there . . .

To hold on until the awakening. That's where you want us to be.

Tonight I have doubts about my mental balance.

[03/05/1994] Saturday.

What R. touched on yesterday in his little talk represents a barrier, a certain poverty. Was mine a reaction of self-love cut to the quick? And was it an illusion to call on You?

Only being detached from everything will allow me (us) to hold fast here until you return, thanks to your Love.

The Tabernacle as *home port*, yes, as long as it does not become a *port of attachment*.[17] It's the Presence of the greatest detachment.

I was not able to see R.'s poverty, who at bottom cannot imagine himself elsewhere, having to invent something else (and perhaps he is also attached to A.).

What You say is: "I am going away," and it's from this that we must draw the source of our strength to be here until, quite simply "you return."

Presence of him who is loved Elsewhere and even further away, for Jesus wants us in his *I am*.

You did not choose sides. You joined neither the Zealots nor the Pharisees nor Pilate's party. You kept your freedom of movement, manifesting the Name, in which you kept your friends.

[03/06/1994] Third Sunday of Lent, 1994.

You cannot put up with trafficking in your Father's house, the house of grace.

The Presence cannot be turned into coin. What is involved is You, risen, here.

17. Brother Christophe is here playing with the phrases *port d'attache* (the ordinary expression for "home port") and his own fanciful *port d'attachement* ("port of attachment").

At Vigils: the God who fills me with courage. It's You, Father, who fill me with weakness and madness, with power: for the ordinariness of a simple existence.

Yesterday with Moussa, hoeing the onions. He says: "You see: Célestin has become like an Algerian and he wants to return to his country. But here there are others—Algerians—who want to destroy this country."

Jesus serene? Zeal for your house will consume me. Anguished to death . . . , your serenity is that of one who prays. Lifting your eyes to heaven, you say: the hour has come, FATHER.

In your Prayer, all human anguish is overcome: by the GIFT that wholly supports your freedom.

The home port is Your Body as the Beloved.

Do not hold me back, for I GO UP to my Father and your Father.

During the night of December 24–25, we passed over from the home to the BODY.

[03/07/1994] Monday.

Jesus, flee, my beloved

you, my port of ultimate and unceasing detachment, launch my heart into the deep

and keep a DEEP LIFE alive in me.

Journey to Algiers: to bring back the benches the White Sisters are giving us since they're moving. I celebrate the Eucharist on this feast of Felicity and Perpetua: that we also may receive the grace to live and die in the only LOVE.

The Gospel traces the only way [*tarîq*, in Arabic in the text]. *The servant is not above his master*: if they have persecuted me . . .

But: "When the Defender, the Breath of truth, comes, he will testify for me."

[03/12/1994] Saturday 12th.

Is it *'Eid,* or the last day of Ramadan? It is love you desire . . .

Christian is back. I feel good about it, and am truly happy. This week in his place has let me feel my limits in trying to embrace each brother and myself. But Jesus leads me little by little, moves me toward the place of being loved. It's in my interest to let myself be led by the act of the Cross: his *I love you* with a mad love. Father Bernardo was speaking to me when he said to Christian (at Timadeuc[18]): "The Order needs monks more than martyrs!" To be taken as it was said: with humor and humility.

The letter from the Ministry of Foreign Affairs, addressed to the papal nuncio, and the question of closing the house still up in the air, tell us again to be here as if ready to leave, in total detachment, the better and the more to offer Your Presence here.

We have sown tomatoes, eggplants, peppers and flowers for your GARDEN.

When will you come down, FRIEND, into your garden?

[03/13/1994] The 13th.

Your Day: for us and for our joy. Your joy in us, full.

And the day of *'Eid al-Fitr.*[19]

Ever since Vigils we have been plunged into the religion of the other. The loudspeaker is unavoidable (solemn call to prayer, then cassette player), and now the chanted and rhythmic repetition of the Name: God is greater, No Divinity but God [*Allah Akbar, la ilâha illa Allah,* in Arabic in the text]. Invoking God as always greater leads the believer to submission. But the image can take your place: an illusory greatness that is only the reflection of a will to power, to revenge also, for the crushed and the humiliated. It was while clamoring your Name that they slaughtered our Croatian brothers and so many others of their own Algerian and Muslim brothers and sisters.

Jesus teaches us to whisper, to sigh, to weep: "Abba, ever greater Papa," with LOVE. In Mary: the Name is pronounced.

18. Monastery of Trappist monks in Brittany.

19. "Festival of breaking of the fast," also called the Sugar Feast and the Lesser *'Eid*. An important religious holiday celebrated by Muslims worldwide. It marks the end of Ramadan, the Islamic holy month of fasting.

Last Thursday I read the following by Bernard, speaking to his monks on Psalm 90, verse 15:

> "His glory is present invisibly, brothers, concealed from us in tribulation. In the momentary character of tribulation, eternity is invisibly present; in the lightness of tribulation is the weight of glory that is beyond all measure." (*Qui habitat* 17.3)

And Brother Pierre-Yves explains:

> "The author wants us to understand that salvation will not come as an intrinsic future to remunerate the present, but that the future is already 'latent' in the present, the future that is in the process of being shaped by the very way we live the presence of God in tribulation. " (note 5)

The Presence of "the one who is greater than our heart"
  is somewhere in me
    where you lead me
      it is to be loved
        and this makes me live infinitely.

I met Bernard again this morning in his commentary on the Song of Songs: "My Beloved is for me a bouquet of myrrh lying between my breasts. Thus, the Spouse does not say that her beloved is a bunch of myrrh, but a simple bouquet, since out of love for him she is ready to find light all the sufferings that will be inflicted on her. It is really a small bouquet, since he is born as a little child among us and the sufferings of this life are as nothing compared to the glory that will be revealed to us one day" (Rom 8:18).

For us as well, what today is a small bouquet of myrrh will one day become infinite glory. Isn't it with reference to this bouquet that the yoke is sweet and the burden light? Not that it is light in itself—the throes of the passions and the sadness of death are not a slight thing—but a loving heart bears them without sorrow.

Since I love, for me it's a bouquet. If she calls him her Beloved now, it's to show that the strength of love outweighs the greatest sufferings, for love is strong as death.

A beautiful Eucharist. On your word, Jesus, I have received the GIFT, the Gift that gives you. I've received it the way one receives a kiss: the better part . . . by stealth. I have grasped it and will never let it go. To obey is to commune in the Gift.

"Do you know that I have the power of killing you?" says the executioner. And the martyr replies: "Do you know that I have the power of being killed?" Christian reminded us of these words of Etty, stressing also the fact that, in Arabic, "to choose" and "good" have the same root—this when the leader affirmed: "You have no choice."

What's at stake here is your freedom.

The important thing, Etty used to say, is not to survive no matter what, but what meaning we give our life.

Gustave Thibon,[20] whom I read this afternoon, guides me to the Man of Sorrows . . . "death by being torn apart."

And to hear the voice of Simone Weil:[21] "Soon there will be a distance between us. Let us love this distance, wholly woven by friendship, for those who love each other are not separated. . . . For we have the happiness of having been thrown by birth at the very foot of the Cross."

I have taken the cup. I have drunk the Unknown of Your ETERNAL LIFE.

[03/14/1994] Monday.

After Vigils, I read and embrace the Gospel: John 9. "Go and wash in the Pool of Siloam (a name that means 'sent')." And obey-

20. Gustave Thibon (1903–2001), French Catholic philosopher.

21. Simone Weil (1909–1942), well-known French Jewish social activist, anarchist, philosopher, and mystic, in deep communion with the Catholic faith even though she never converted.

ing leads to seeing: You who speak to me. To see my brother at last as a subject who speaks: a face where the Word unveils itself.

I go look up the actual text Etty wrote in the camp at Westerbork: "What matters, in fact, is not to stay alive at any cost [and this is what we have unanimously excluded by refusing to pay], but *how* we stay alive. Sometimes it seems to me that every new situation, whether better or worse, carries in itself the possibility of enriching a person with new intuitions."

And earlier I had already copied the rest of this text in a notebook:

> "And if we let fate decide the heavy realities that irrevocably confront us—if we do not offer them a shelter in our hearts and minds so as to allow them there a space to clarify and transform themselves into elements of maturity, into substances from which we can extract a significance—this would mean that our generation is not armed for living." (p. 37)

And further: (to offer) this new meaning, gushing forth from the deepest abyss of our distress and hopelessness.

[03/15/1994] Tuesday.

Christian went to see R. yesterday afternoon.

Before Vespers I met Ali in Your garden, ensconced in this space of greenery and air. He talks to me about what has happened to him, what he has seen, heard, touched. No ideological or even plain conceptual reflex. I don't understand all the words. I hear his deep emotion, his interior upheaval and immense distress: "It's as if you're out in the ocean with waves. First you're thrown one way, then the other. You're at the mercy of it. . . ." Ezekiel speaks of water today and that's also an experience: the experience of the current is given only to the one who gets into the water. "A swimmer with a single love" (Georges Sali).

[03/16/1994] Wednesday.

The Gift seizes your body—otherwise it is an idea of a gift.

To lose my life, that is the Gift: take it or leave it.

At chapter yesterday evening, I clearly heard a brother say that he did not want any aggressiveness at the meeting for mutual aid that we're considering. It is, in fact, very difficult to help someone who is aggressive.

[03/18/1994] Friday.

"Lord, as we move from the past toward what is new, we beg you: make us leave behind what can only grow old and put in us a spirit of renewal and holiness" (Prayer after Communion).

In the garden with Mohammed, just back from Blida, where he saw three murdered men lying on the sidewalk. He says to me: "If we remember Him, He protects us. . . . You see, I crossed the checkpoints without any problem."

This evening we begin the solemnity of Saint Joseph, but in poor shape. Christian and W. are in Algiers, and Jean-Pierre is sick: his face is swollen, he's exhausted, but still a faithful . . . and suffering servant.

[03/19/1994] March 19th. Feast of Saint Joseph.

Today I hear deep inside myself your happiness at being in me: You, Love's Beloved.

That experience of poverty—so pathetic that you don't know whether to laugh or to cry—by that student from Tours saying *I love you* without any response forthcoming.

It is your *I love you* that draws me to the reciprocity of the Gift.

Your freedom, Jesus, is the freedom of your attraction:

where I walk
behind you
there we are: the point is to follow you.

[03/20/1994] The 20th.

Your new day finds me a bit grumpy despite the springtime.

To serve, to follow, and: "where I am, there also will my servant be."

You are here: you go.

In the house of Islam—in the present state of its Algerian structuring (!)—it's probably not opportune to present oneself as . . . the house across the road—structured differently . . .

It's better to be the Body of your Presence resolutely and simply, to be simply there in a relationship of love—vulnerable, exposed.

When it's a question of being monks here, this body—according to the best hypothesis—would be characterized by . . . its wide-open ears, its gaze, its Nazarene-Trappist accent: and its child's size. The Father is GREATER.

[03/22/1994] The 22nd.

Lord Jesus, your friend—this country you love—is sick. And we, and me too, sick with love's wounds.

This sickness, you say, will not end in death.

You shudder. You are distressed.

Lazarus! Come out!

Unbind him, let him WALK.

The following explains M.'s reaction this morning: two youths, 17 and 24 years old, brutally tortured, then executed by law-enforcement officials (?) during the night. I said: "You know, I cannot choose those who kill." He answers me sharply, emotional but sure of himself: "You cannot say that, *you ought not* to choose." And I insisted—doubtless it was a mistake—by adding: "I choose this: they can kill me." Ali heard me. "Oh, no!"

[03/23/1994] The 23rd.

One is so quickly caught up in this illusory alternative between opposite types of violence.

Disciples: the truth shall make us—me too, Jesus, please—free men here.

No one takes my life in his own camp and making threats: I lay it down, I divest myself of it.

May my life here no longer belong to me. I am not here to defend Christian ideas, an ideological truth that can so easily turn exclusive. (Just now in Algiers there was an Algerian woman, member of the democratic party, on Channel III, denouncing fundamentalism and allowing it no room in the Algeria that she desires and is fighting for.)

What remains for us is the freedom of hostages: not the freedom to escape, but the freedom of the person who goes beyond it all, breaking through the imprisonment imposed by all forms of violence. In the Father's house there are many rooms.

[03/24/1994] The 24th.

In chapter before Compline, Christian informs us that two Frenchmen have been killed in Algiers. In the morning, Brother Luc talked to me about Socrates, Gandhi, and Jean d'Ormesson.[22] "I don't give a damn about death, and I'm not afraid of either the terrorists or the police." And . . . what I look to is You, Jesus. Your distress when facing death, both Lazarus' death and the one coming to take you. What matters is to be joined to you: "The one who keeps my word shall never see death." You make me go beyond the idea, the image, of death. You exempt me from having to imagine myself a hero or a martyr. That is beyond me. It is enough (and I beg you for this) not to be separated from You as You GO forward.

Before First Vespers of the Annunciation, read X.'s letter. I realize how much, deep within me, I was waiting to hear his VOICE. I believe that I have run towards him, as in Luke 15. This doesn't mean I'm forgetting what in me resembles the older

22. Jean d'Ormesson (b. 1925), French novelist, chronicler, editor (notably of *Le Figaro*), actor, and philosopher, member of the Académie Française.

brother who wasn't happy when the younger left, resentful at being abandoned by him in that way.

The attitudes that emerge from this letter make me happy because of you and your grace. It's also a terrific challenge to live, to hold on to your Presence, without being attached to how specifically this might happen.

Tomorrow we're going down to Algiers with Michel, for the meeting of the diocesan priests.

I tell Moussa that X. has written to me. He says: "Oh, that's good news, that's really good news. You must give me his address."

[03/27/1994] March 27th. Palm (Passion) Sunday.

Jesus is the master of events: of what happens to us here.

And if they ask you: "What are you doing here?" answer that the Master has need of it.

And they let them carry on.

Jesus, facing the violence in the narrative of his Passion, in Mark.

The violence that kills is not what many people say it is these days: things people disguise or excuse or justify as the necessary means we must go through.

It is a deliberate, motivated decision to make one or more people die.

Jesus' way of confronting it is to make us sit down at table.

When facing a murderous decision, this is the space that resists and holds out: a place of essential conviviality, exchange, sharing.

And then something happens: a woman comes in and performs a foolish act that professes her love there in front of everybody. Love for the Beloved.

Like that man at Bologhine who picked up a policeman, wounded by a terrorist, who was lying in the middle of the road; he got him into his car and drove him to the hospital—and saved his life.

And was himself murdered a week later.

Jesus does not accuse Judas—he does not name him—he only reveals the lie. He proposes the truth. This, and not any one of us, is what stares down the decision to murder: everyone flees.

What makes us hold firm is holding on to Jesus, communing with the Gift in Act: a resolution of Love.

Jesus stands there, facing the violence aimed at him, and says: as for me, I'm going to pray. Anguish. Still he says: "Abba!"

To face murder there's only interior childhood in its indestructible relation to Abba. Jesus obeys and leaps in—and we along with him.

Onward! Stand up!

Over against the armed gang, Jesus counters with what he is: the Word. He speaks.

[03/29/1994] Tuesday in Holy Week.

I wrote to my bishop yesterday, "reacting" to his project on communication for the African Synod: "A mission for the Church: to promote evangelical relations with Muslims." I am very ambivalent about a mission expressed like that. Me, a promoter? Of values, products, ideas, systems, morals? It's an enterprise doomed to fail: the competition on the market of religions is far too disloyal here.

It's elsewhere I feel called to abide until your return: in the place where I can offer your Presence and receive it.

Our Gospel mission: to live the Good News of our relation with Muslims. It's up to the Church to believe in Christ-like relations here today.

Today we're going to work in the vineyard. Tie up the pruned branches. I'm going to ponder all this: You, planted here in this land of Algeria

and without you nothing can be done (that perdures)
you: bear in us fruits of friendship.
I pray to the Father that this may come to pass
among us
the GIFT
that's stronger than the murder.

[03/30/1994] Wednesday.

M. and Mohammed speak to me about the approaching feast they so await. They are waiting for the Fire of paschal love.

My Father is the vine-dresser. Today we continue tying up the branches that have "burst." Bursts of life. Rush of Christ-sap. It's a job for believers; the lambs come out to pasture in the vineyard, and as for its future fruit: uncertainty and threats weigh it down.

[03/31/1994] Holy Thursday.

I have just said to her: Mary, I love you.

It's meaningless. It is "pure" fabrication. But at least it doesn't hurt anyone. Is it naïveté? No. It is true. It's in the Breath of truth. It's communion in the flesh of the Son:

in his *I love you* of flesh and blood.

pure Breath   lead me toward the full truth

of what I say to the Church

Mary, I love you,

Let it be ever truer

every day, here: for my brothers, for Mohammed, Moussa, Ali, Sami, Salim and all the others.

Concerning Jesus' words "I shall see you again," Xavier-Léon Dufour[23] says that John transposes, substitutes and makes the gazing coincide with the coming

its reciprocity comes to us from You.

[04/01/1994] Friday.

A people about to be born: that is your work, Jesus.

I find the table again: you prepare it for us in the sight of our foes: it is for them as well.

23. Xavier-Léon Dufour (1912–2007), French Jesuit biblical scholar and theologian.

To believe is to consent to your return to the Father. This consent opens my heart to the Gift that makes me dwell wherever you go, where your I AM is *I love you* and openly communicates the Father, Abba, to me.

Courage, you say, I have overcome the world. Lord, lead all the faithful to where you are disarmed: sunk in prayer, handed over, surrendered to Love.

Only Odette and Gilles are with us to celebrate your Passion of Love.

Communion with You who are going away. Christian speaks to us about the Innocent One. This morning Mohammed explained his prayer to him this way: My God, we have done nothing evil, pardon us, forgive us.

And Jesus says: "Father, forgive them." And give us Mary, the Innocent One, to let us be born made innocent again.

Moussa joined me this morning in weeding a seedbed: ". . . and in my heart too there is good and evil." Who said Muslims have no sense of sin?

[04/02/1994] And Saturday.

Toward me, your desire: of LIFE.

In me, toward the Father: you go. Flee, Beloved!

Yesterday Ali gave us bread through Z., a friend of Brother Luc.

It was Ali I met in the garden when I went to water it, and Ali who offered me your presence there after the reading of your Passion.

[04/03/1994] Easter, today, here, with You.

If I go back to last night, it's because it's truly there it happens: You,

the event of your *I love you.*

I went to sleep before Vigils to gather strength for the chant I had to contribute. I had this dream: I was making signs to Ben Ali not to answer me, not to come and talk to me. He approaches smiling. He goes away again and is caught by the police. He is tortured. Afterwards, there's the Fire in spite of the curfew. It's a beautiful and simple celebration, truly steeped in faith and prayer. Christian's role as presider brings forth fruits of unity and makes the Event truly present. I encounter again the mystery of the short ending of Mark's Gospel, because of the way Christian deciphered and commented on it while re-reading a letter from Claire. What an overwhelming experience, and the "lump in my throat" . . . out of fear of the essential words.

Yes, Jesus needs to go through our flesh in order to express himself as the Living Risen One. Faith is to begin with the Word: to speak truly, to speak openly. It's the whole existence of the *I love you* enacted.

Gilles presides at today's Eucharist. He evokes the shaken and threatened faith . . . , and the wavering of the disciple who was the most intelligent of them all (and the fastest runner): he saw and believed. Gilles speaks of the LIFE that is definitive. I let that word work me over. Infinitive and definitive. What does that mean to me?

[04/04/1994] Monday.

The Gospel (Mt 28:8-15) tells me today that the encounter with the Risen One takes place on the road, after we've left the empty tomb. And we run . . . and you come. That's what happens to the women, and that's what you say to them about us: "Tell my brothers they are to go into Galilee, there they will see me."

To see you here.

Blessed the pure in heart, those who hope.

What perdures and is full of future promise are not Christian values that might be promoted (with a new outlay of funds) by a very threatened institution; rather, it's this little group of men and women who are joined to you. Standing upright. When people are being killed all around, and those few receive your Breath so that your relationship with all may be lived here: your new commandment.

Sooner or later, this Relationship with You (that is opening a network of other relationships—a communion) is going to collide with a religious totalitarianism that cannot but reject such freedom, such openness, such a breach in the dividing wall, which defy its fundamentalist shutdown, its deceitful order.

[04/05/1994] Tuesday.

Last night we chanted: "Arise, O God, defend your cause / remember those madmen who blaspheme all day long."

"Madmen" is what Mohammed calls them, when at Tlemcen he lamented: *they have understood nothing*. Nevertheless, in me, in him, in us that madness may meet up with a willing accomplice, coward, traitor or turncoat. We need the stronger madness of the Love on the Cross.

Today: Jn 20:11-18. *Mariam. Rabbouni.*

The infinite dialogue is reconnected. The presence is found anew. All it takes is to turn around: and suddenly you're Love standing there.

Yesterday morning, I read Maurice Bellet's[24] beautiful book: *Au Christ inconnu* ["To the Unknown Christ"]. It finishes like this: "But knowing Christ always sends us back to the beginning. His place is in Genesis (the Garden). That is why to know him is to be born again, to make our own what he himself is: the always-new birth of true man.

"(. . .) our life is first death

"(. . .) we are each other's violence

"(. . .) But don't you see, my friend, that here it is the opposite?

"Don't you see that, if I don't cease to look at the Crucified, it's because here I see life triumphant transfiguring this ultimate death?

"It's true, we believe the unbelievable: that what is the utterly inaccessible comes to us is this imperishable love that I

24. Maurice Bellet (b. 1923), French priest, writer, philosopher, and theologian with a psychoanalytical emphasis.

scarcely dare to name, since our language has become all baseness and mockery.

"And what is the proof, you say, what is the proof? None other than this: living is possible."

[04/11/1994] Monday, April 11th.

The Octave of Easter is finished, whew! It was difficult—painful. I am undoubtedly still too rich interiorly to live well those moments of tiredness, tension, irritation and frustration. Saturday there was the fit of anger against our neighbor and his sheep, then against Mohammed. Where was then the good news of fraternal relations? When I manage to go beyond such angry reactions, then I can sense this Gospel thrust all the stronger which allows me to look at Mohammed and receive his honest gaze. He doesn't judge me. "You know, I didn't notice a thing." My explanations, my reasons have their place, but they fall so short of the essence of what transpired between us out there—something given. I do believe it came from you.

"Where would we go, Lord?" The question is permanently being asked within us. It keeps going right through us ever since the encounter. We live with it, I think, pretty well, each one according to his temperament. What Peter says—there, standing before you—remains inseparable from the same question experienced in reality:

"To whom would we go, Lord?"
Your word here makes us live for ever
Your word makes us live always
your Word in us goes out to others, and your word in them comes forth to us.

To whom would we go . . . it's almost a decision to leave,
but it's been put off until later: Your word makes us live here
so we stay, we abide. Come, Lord—O You!—here.

[04/14/1994] Thursday, April 13th.

In our Easter mail: X. "My dearest brothers of Atlas, [. . .] I really wanted to say to you also these words of Saint Paul: 'For he is our peace, and has made the two peoples into one and broken down the barrier which used to keep them apart, actually destroying in his own person the hatred caused by the rules and decrees of the Law. This was to create one single New Man in himself out of the two of them, and by restoring peace through the cross, to unite them both in a single Body and reconcile them with God. In his own person he killed the hatred' (Eph 2:14-16). Yes, peace and joy! Know that I remain united with you in prayer and affection."

And from Canada, Ahmed Ben Ali says: "For me, *my family are my friends*. It is a door open on to infinity. It's a hand reached out to help climb a path in the high mountain where the feast has already begun. It's an inestimable jewel. It's an eternal flower that we have the happiness to contemplate together. . . ."

And also D.M.

Near you—you who are so close to Him who calls you
Woman
Near his Cross I am
in the future of this *I love you* yet to come.

Here, Ahmed saw that the family (of Jesus Christ) are his friends.

[04/16/1994] Saturday.

"It is I. Do not be afraid" [*anâ huwa la takhâfû*, in Arabic in the text].

The "modality" of our presence in Algeria finds its kenotic inspiration here: "No one takes my life, I myself let go of it":

this—us here—
is my body
where hatred finds what is stronger than itself: it is
killed.

[04/19/1994] The 19th.

You in whom I believe
toward whom I am coming. Friend: I am coming
to where you draw me
(I have my return ticket).

[04/20/1994] Wednesday.

To hear you say to me: I am the bread of life,
and to come to you quickly to live here today.

"To see the Son": is this what is happening to me? The proof is not in a vision, but perhaps simply in my eyes in expectancy, on a journey, in prayer (you alone know), in tears.

Maurice Bellet, *Le point critique* ["The Critical Point"], p. 232. We are actually afraid of what the Gospel says to us, afraid of the anguish it can lead us to, and that's why we reduce it to a banal "religious language" that does not touch reality at all. But the Gospel is an infinitely difficult book, for the person who reads it with open eyes, who has achieved the second naïveté and has become "like a child."

[04/22/1994] The 22nd.

Maria Gabriella.[25] *Mia sorella* ["my little sister"]: Dare I ask you . . . for your helping hand? You succeeded in giving your life. Will I get to that point: today?

[04/23/1994] Saturday.

"This saying is hard; who can hear it?"

25. Blessed Maria Gabriella Sagheddu (1914–1939) was a Trappistine nun. She was born in Sardinia and died of tuberculosis in Grottaferrata. She offered her life to God for the cause of Christian unity and was beatified by John Paul II in 1983. Her shrine is at the Trappistine monastery of Vitorchiano, where the community of Grottaferrata was transferred.

What you say endures, holds . . . and you can even take your departure from the "place" where you have spoken—language made man—to return to Him who is the origin of what you say: Abba.

You have left. You have gone up toward Him by the ladder that was raised there. And what you have said continues to be said whenever any man or woman believes to the point of saying to you: "Rabbi, to whom would we go? You have words of eternal life." Your word gives life forever.

Such are your last words to Mary and then to the disciple, and they give me life, here, forever.

We had foreseen the possibility of leaving, of having to leave the place.

What remains is this profound movement of going toward you. Then we must leave everything.

To be a disciple monk here leads to dispossession, to detachment.

How could we not be dispossessed by so much distress all around? And by Joy: strange, wild, free: your joy, here, inculturated.

Onward! Today: to the VINEYARD.

[04/25/1994]

Yesterday, on Good Shepherd Sunday, at Terce: I bombed out, unable to carry on as cantor. Suddenly I didn't have a single note in my head. I withdrew to the side of the laity and stayed there like an idiot, but: You were there, in the midst of that very fragile "us" . . . so beautiful, so difficult to live in truth.

Christian slips me some news from X. [. . .] He's made up his mind: he is coming back here. We'll find the right way to do it. I'm happy and at peace about this: good news. Onwards, then!

[04/30/1994] April 30th.

Our Lady of Africa (Jn 19:25-27). Beautiful Mass, Jean-Pierre tells me.

[05/01/1994] May 1st. Fifth Sunday of Easter.

I am the true vine,
my Father is the vine-dresser.
We have finished weeding: the vineyard of the fathers.
They hold on to it with a mysterious attachment.

I have jotted this down on a piece of paper: What perdures here, what is full of future promise, is not Christian values, even if they are promoted at enormous expense (but with what personnel?); no, what holds is the relationship with Christ.

The relation between the branches and the vine. Without you nothing can be done here. In you: we bear fruit, become disciples.

In the Acts of the Apostles, I read that the Church (or, according to another text, the Churches) was being built up and growing.

Constancy, permanence, stability . . . and then: mobility, the road.

Both "Abide!" and " Let's go forward!"

Christian gives me a letter to read that he's received from X.

[05/03/1994] The 3rd.

Feast day of Philippe (from Tamié): I'll soon see him there. His ordination will surely do something for our friendship. I'm supposed to say some words on that blessed day.

[05/04/1994] The 4th.

You phoned me here, and I was moved to hear by your voice. The voice of a friend.

As you know, I'm not very familiar with that gadget and perhaps not very gifted either in communicating; but the bond between us has been established by someone else, and it's stronger than death.

Yes, I've already told you. It's simply this: I'm really happy to be going to this event—your ordination. I am going as a friend, and if there's something to be said, I think I shall speak.

During lunch Pascale calls me. . . . Again strong feelings on both sides.

May the Spirit come: the reign of Communion.

Mohammed has not looked well these past couple of days. But we had a good heart-to-heart nevertheless. Yesterday I learnt the "reason": his wife is sick—"She cries. She's in pain . . . ," but he's the hardest hit. The Good News is at home between those two, and for me it's to be found there as their brother.

[05/06/1994] The 6th.

Terrible repression around us. The epicenter is your cross, where you let go of your life for the sake of those whom you love: here, today.

[05/08/1994] The 8th.

At 2 p.m., at the Ben Shnets center in the Kasbah, Henri Vergès, a Marist brother, and Paule-Hélène, a little Sister of the Assumption, were assassinated. "No one has greater love than the one who lets go of his life for the sake of those he loves."

[05/10/1994] The 10th.

Prayer ought to guide my whole daily existence toward the hour of passing from this world to the Father.

What you say draws me here. How greatly our Church clings to you: to your Spirit of truth. You send her the Defender, and in the death of Paule-Hélène and Henri he unmasks the Lie. He makes us standing firm and endure: at this very work station where your own Love kept them, giving themselves there to the limit. This testimony passes through servants and friends; but it comes from afar, it goes and commingles with the Eucharist.

[05/11/1994] Wednesday.

They are worried about our safety at the *wilayah*[26] headquarters. Christian meets some people there and tells them that here is where we are "most" secure. To leave Tibhirine would mean to leave Algeria behind. Which is what I am going to do for a few days.

Today, your Gospel says that you still have many things to say: to whom? To us here, today, to the world. Paule-Hélène and Henri said something about this, and it is *you*: language made man.

The Breath of truth: he will communicate to you what is to come. He will liberate us from fear, since nothing can happen to us from the outside which is imposed and excludes choice.

Everything that happens to us—our presence here at Tibhirine as well as all simple and fraternal things—comes to us from You by the Gift that is at work in us: and that has its effect much further than "us": opening the house of Prayer to everybody.

[06/01/1994] June 1st.

I have returned to where your Love sustains us: alive.

From May 13th to the 30th, you led me. You guided my steps. You watched over me from my departure to my return. I received much Love. Help me to keep nothing of it for myself. We have given everything, Henri said on May 1st. I am happy to be here. Each one, in his own way, gives signs of marked fatigue.

[06/02/1994] June 2nd.

R. here. I like to be here. *I love you* here.

Some theologians suggest that all religions in the world constitute a "unitive pluralism" or a "coincidence of opposites," each one contributing a "unique and complementary character." Each religion and each religious figure are unique and *definitive* for those who follow them (*cf.* the theology of Islam); but they are

26. *Wilayah:* an administrative division in Arab countries, usually translated as "province," governed by a *wali* or "provincial governor."

also of *universal* interest for the other religions. In other words, the unique character is neither exclusive ("against") nor inclusive ("in" or "above"), but essentially *relative* ("with") with regard to the other religions.

[06/03/1994] The 3rd.

Consequently, there are not only numerous routes to the summit of Mount Fuji, but these numerous routes should cross each other and get information from one another if they all want to reach the end of their journey. [. . .] There is more in the Logos-Christ than in the historical Christ.

Ecclesiocentrism → Christocentrism → Theocentrism . . .

It is no longer the Church (to the extent that it is necessary for salvation) nor Christ (as normative for salvation), but God as divine Mystery who is present at the center of the history of salvation and is the starting point of interreligious dialogue.

Anniversary of my ordination to the diaconate in 1989.

[06/05/1994] The 5th.

"God has really spoken in Jesus and this message ought to be heard by all. But 'really' does not necessarily mean 'only'. Thus, Christians can be totally attached to Jesus Christ and at the same time fully open to a possible message from God in other religions. Or can they?

"A liberation theology with reference to the various religions?

[. . .] "Beginning with the preferential option for the poor [. . . , which] suggests that what allows the different religions to speak with each other (dialogue) and understand each other (theology), is their common concern and their different efforts to promote 'salvation' (FIS)[27] or the liberation of all persons, especially those who are poorest and suffer the most [. . .].

27. FIS: French acronym for "Islamic Salvation Front" *(Front Islamique de Salut).* Algerian militant religious and political movement for the purpose of founding an Islamic state in Algeria. Officially dissolved in 1992.

"The praxis is at the same time the origin and the confirmation of the theory or doctrine. All beliefs and affirmations of truth by Christians ought to develop from their praxis, or from the lived experience of these truths, and ought to be reconfirmed by this same practice and experience. Applied to a theology of religions, this means that Christians can proclaim that Jesus is the definitive and normative Word of God for all religions solely in and by the practice of dialogue with the other religions. It is only in an encounter like this that one may experience and confirm what is normative in Christ."[28]

Feast of your Body   you give us what has to be done
Feast of your Blood   here, today.

The army is surrounding Tibhirine.

Last night before Vespers a family showed up in which both mother and father are doctors, with little Meriem, three months old, in her mother's arms, and her "big" sister. They say: "How can we leave?" In the morning, traveling by car, they see three corpses on the road and say: "Let them fight it out among themselves. That's not our business."

Christian talked to me about us as hostages. Yes, but we must live this experience identified with the little people, with a view to LIBERATION and with the very FREEDOM of Jesus Christ: "No one can take my life."

In your presence I want to recall the faces encountered between May 13th and the 30th.

On the flight from Algiers to Orly there was a doctor, registered in medical school. He spoke to me of his first attraction to the FIS and to the imam's sermons and of his disappointment with Pasqua's[29] measures in France. A sad, disoriented and rather confused man.

28. Paul Knitter, in *Concilium*, no. 203 (1986), 135–36.

29. Charles Pasqua, French interior minister (1993–1995) who spearheaded severe anti-immigration laws.

Then, at Orly, there were Vincent, Thérèse, Marie-Annick. Then an hour at Madame de Chergé's[30] home: we spoke all about my life in Algeria. Prayer together. In the evening, Micède. In Rennes, Father Sébastien. At Campénéac,[31] Mother Geneviève, very human, all woman. Then at Timadeuc, Brother Yann (novice master). Louis-Marie (guest master). François-Xavier, who's set on coming here. In the evening, supper with Father Abbot Paul. Yvonne and Michel.

Between Timadeuc and Nantes, I go to the family of Brother Michel at Pont-Château. I meet Marie-France and Louis and others there; I get the impression of a real family. I am there simply as a brother. In Nantes, Madeleine and Jacky receive us. I spend the evening and the night with Yvonne and Michel at La Roche-sur-Foron, with early morning Mass there. At Bellefontaine[32] I meet Célestin, who gives me a tour of the monastery during which I run into different brothers in the refectory and the laundry. Brother Yvon is in the infirmary. And then there was Father Joseph Lépine.

Train from Angers to Tours: Pascale and Simon (with his bag!). Caroline and Cédric at Vendôme. Juliette and Bastienne, and then Martin. In Morec, Aunt Yvette and François. Evening at the home of Yves and Annick: there, Chantale and J.-F., Florence and Marie-Paule (Michel).

TGV[33] from Vendôme to Paris. Needy people asking for money. I give some to one Bosnian woman and say no to another.

At Albertville I meet Claude, who drives me up to Tamié. Jean-Marc, Didier, Danièle Maire. Gérard T. asks: "So you're still holding on to life, then?" "No: I am already in LIFE."

I preside at the Eucharist on Friday and am moved. "Do you love me?" A creative, liberating question that opens each heart to reply.

30. Mother of Father Christian de Chergé, prior of Tibhirine.
31. Monastery of Trappistine nuns in Brittany.
32. Monastery of Trappist monks in the Vendée region.
33. TGV: acronym for "Train à Grande Vitesse" (high-speed train).

A certain solitude: the community and the brothers, like me, have continued on their way. I remember that something important had been decided within me at Tamié, and now I retrieve it—this vivid memory—in the cloister, before the tabernacle, while speaking with Gérard, and in the refectory.

Philippe greets me at the beginning of Vespers. We talk together during the great silence after Compline. Words are exchanged in a truly fraternal way. I can breathe again. I had been a little anxious.

Philippe's ordination. I'm a part of the ceremony. This is happening to me. A special place is reserved for me as friend, since I'm to speak. I go up to the altar where Philippe is concelebrating next to Bishop Marcel. A beautiful ceremony with chants, instrumental music, flowers, all very human.

Bertrand came this morning. We talked. He tells me that he came back to the FAITH when I "decided" to become a priest. Suzanne T.

Pentecost: arrival in Ancône. I am full of the faces I've seen. [. . .]

Masses in different homes, opening the house where Your Love is at work: a little church where I am very happy. [. . .]

At Blauvac[34] with Jacques A., Father Étienne, Georges. Mass with Jacques: we concentrate on the essential by being faithful to your original Gesture.

A long phone call from X. [. . .]

Thursday: Aiguebelle.[35] Brother Placide. Dom Aelred. [. . .] Evening at the visitors' house: the Bonpains, the Lebretons. [. . .]

Friday: Marie-Christine. Mass.

Saturday: Saint-Paul-Trois-Châteaux. Brother Cyprien at Aiguebelle.

Sunday: Mass in the parish. Festive lunch for Mothers' Day.

With Fr. and Zabeth to Marseilles to see J.B.: The Center (Christian, Joseph, Philippe—I don't dare). Eucharist on Monday

34. Monastery of Trappistine nuns in Provence.
35. Monastery of Trappist monks in the Dauphiné.

in J.B.'s room. L'(?). Paulette. Bruno. Mireille. Marc Marignane: Jean-François.

Algiers: (100°F.!): Paul. On the road. Military personnel. Tibhirine: Christian, Ali.

[06/06/1994] Monday.

A lasting, almost insistent impression of being loved. If it would only pierce me through and through.

[06/07/1994] Tuesday.

You draw me to where I am loved. My resistance melts little by little.

This is really what stays with me from my journey to France, and that makes me feel moved, touched, overwhelmed: being loved. Thus maybe Algeria has in fact been loved through what I have been able to witness about her and her suffering.

I said to Christian: I am a postulant for the Ribât.[36]

Who would be able to perform a work of reconciliation here today? You.

At Mass, after the Gospel and the reading (from 1 Kings) about the widow of Zarephath, I read the poem "The Well" by Jean-Claude Renard:

> *But how can we affirm it's already too late*
> *to fulfill the desire—*
> *so patient does the gift remain;*
> *and when always, perhaps, something or*
> *someone says, from of the depth of silence and nakedness,*
> *that an ineffable fire continues to dig in us*
> *beneath wastelands peopled by thorns*
> *a well that nothing exhausts.*

36. Ribât ("keeping watch"): Movement for Islamic-Christian encounters, initiated by the community of Tibhirine. It brought together Christians (both religious and lay) and Sufi Muslims.

[06/08/1994] Wednesday.

Bruno and Yiaha driven from the Birsa by a member of the GIA.[37] To be continued . . .

[06/12/1994] Sunday.

Impatience and aggressiveness not held in check during the Office. Someone could say to me: "That is neither the time nor the place." Rather: profit from reciting the Psalms and allow yourself to go beyond those feelings, until we receive the strength to say the Our Father together. At Lauds, this struck me from the reading: "the stretching out of days."

yes we have come to this
in the stretching out of days,
   uncertainly
in the duration of your body
   so humiliated
in the story of your will
   so infinitely set
   and resolved
   to love
      us   here

[06/13/1994] Monday 13th.

Disturbances in choir.

To persevere with a steady voice. I've been asked to serve in this position, and I shouldn't try to get out of it too quickly.

"But *I say* to you: Do not resist the evil one." Your voice irrupts there in our midst and *says*

just as God *says* Himself, tells Himself

37. GIA: French acronym for "Groupe Islamiste Algérien" ("Algerian Islamist Group"), an Algerian terrorist organization.

with the freedom to *say*: speaking to us in You, his Son, without violence ever being able to influence or modify his language: you give your Word to the very end. There—in this GIFT—resides all his Strength, which is the violence of Love: "But as for me, I *say* to you . . ."

To listen to you Jesus, in this difficulty between us (X. and me). To let go of my aggressive and homicidal retort: because it's you who *say*, and I may hope to be able to slip into your *Saying*, to blend in with your Song (of humility).

[06/14/1994] And Tuesday.

You say to us, you say to me today, in this Algerian *entre nous* in which enemies are practicing *internecine* slaughter: "LOVE your enemies, PRAY FOR your enemies." I hear Silouan: "To pray is to give the blood of one's own heart." And Father Pierre: "The most beautiful prayer that Jesus left us is the CROSS." Silouan again: "The Lord taught me to love my enemies. Deprived of divine grace we cannot love our enemies, but the Holy Spirit teaches us to love. . . . When you pray for your enemies, peace will come upon you."

[06/19/1994] Sunday.

"Be still! . . . and there was a great calm." That's how it is in today's gospel. May it be done to me according to your Saying. This Friday, when called to the guest house to hear a confession, I was overtaken by a great desire to listen and also to free the other person's joy and happiness: she is indeed beloved.

I am reading Christian Bobin:[38] "What saves us does not protect us from anything, and yet it does save us. [. . .] Love, look after yourself."[39]

38. Christian Bobin (b. 1951), French Catholic writer.
39. *L'inespérée* ["The Unexpected"] (Paris: Gallimard, 1994), 108–9.

[06/21/1994] Tuesday 21st.

I sing (in choir) and fall on my face.
You. Love: attentive to the blood being shed.

[06/26/1994] Sunday.

You say to her: "My daughter."

And no one had ever truly said "My daughter" to her in a real face-to-face encounter.

In this way you appeal to the child in me, whenever I do believe in you.

And you continue your liberating utterance: "Your faith has saved you, go in peace and be cured of your illness."

Cured by being recognized, by being loved. And I discover this astounding thing that seems to move you profoundly: my faith, concrete and real.

It is here in Tibhirine that I am a believer in You.

Make me enter into your infinite respect for the faith of the other: even if it is different or even hidden and sick.

Let me share your thirst: your prayer that they may all believe.

To believe: close to the Woman standing there.

[06/28/1994] Tuesday 28th.

Today Amos speaks to me, raging: "Prepare to meet your Lord."

But you appease his words. A great calm comes about, and I hear:

I am preparing you
to meet me.

[07/02/1994] Saturday, July 2nd.

A letter from Mom last Thursday told me about Caroline's death. At the Eucharist in the evening, an amazing closeness. My memory opens up and I receive a sister into Your LIFE. Mysterious communion. Caroline had a hazardous existence, I think. You have sought. You have been found. Give me your free hand, please.

A letter from the nuncio, who is preparing for us to be installed in the nunciature.

I cannot imagine us anywhere but here. This is the place you show us today. On we go!

Since Christmas we have been on the move: free to be here until proven otherwise. Do we have to expect adversity? Perhaps we are still far from the Place of LIFE, from the holy Place . . . of the cross, where the eternal *I love you* (open to everyone) is pronounced in the End.

Neither can our neighbors imagine us anywhere but here, with them. It's with them we have the opportunity of living our monastic vocation and of etching into reality a poor and imperfect response as disciples, as a living Church.

We discuss W. again. The shape of his vocation remains undecided. What's at the bottom of it all? Is there accessibility, . . . "mutual help"?

[07/06/1994] July 6th.

"There was a great calm." I have written down that great calm. . . .

As reader in the refectory, I mediate the voice of Jean-Marie Huret, an unruly worker-priest . . .

One by one
the weapons
fell from my hands
weapons that you yourself had given me one day.
Shred after shred
the tunic disappeared
after the cloak.

Worn smooth? Given away? Torn off?
I don't even know any more
so much does

this unique moment
frighten me now
when two heavy beams
lie before you
lie before me.

Love, O tenderness,
please tell me no more about it.

O Beauty, under thorns and blood
O my God, naked and more resplendent
than all monstrances and their jewel work
let me only draw from your gaze
the strength to follow you
into this remoteness
where night is hiding
behind the stars.

Brother Jacques Rousse

[07/07/1994] July 7th.

You have received everything as pure gift
give everything as pure gift:
this is what it means to consent
(completely and simply) to the Gift.

[07/10/1994] Sunday, July 10th.

Meeting with Christian this morning.
As he is leaving, he refers to death.
And we speak a little about it.

"That is what has changed in me," he tells me: "my relationship with death. It is part of my life. I am struck by what was said by the eye-witnesses to the assassinations at Ben Shnets: the serenity, the calm on the faces of Paule-Hélène and Henri."

Is that a morbid thought? It's within me. I'm not troubled by the fact that one of us—either Christian or myself—is going to die.

[07/11/1994] 07/11. Saint Benedict.

The joy of your call that keeps me here among my brothers. Nine persons murdered in Algiers, seven of them foreigners, at the very time of our Eucharist. I presided. Homily at the hottest time of day. Even so, I talked about eternal life, of following you to your glory . . . , of arriving there together: drawn. Before Compline a difficult chapter. W. speaks up, then some of the others. I brought up "obedience." Where do I myself stand in this respect?

[07/12/1994] The 12th.

Your will: infinitely ample.

At bottom I'm always returning to that *I love you* spoken one day in Tours, and my life is entrusted to that word: it overtakes me, overwhelms me, exceeds me.

Will you tell me, Love, in the End, what you will say to me in my loving misery that remained there, at that point of infinite poverty, when I said

to someone else

I love you.

This morning, I read in Marguerite Porete:[40] "People who have no will at all live in the freedom of charity; [. . .] they have learned to trust in what is beyond them, and the knowledge born of this trust lies in the fact that one can know nothing about it."

The Gift is not an object of knowledge.

[07/14/1994] The 14th.

When he appears, he will unclutter everything: I know nothing more.

40. Marguerite Porete, mystic and author of *The Mirror of Simple Souls*, a work of Christian spirituality dealing with the workings of Divine Love. She was burnt at the stake for heresy in Paris in 1310. The book is sometimes cited as one of the primary texts of the medieval "Heresy of the Free Spirit."

In the refectory last night, the end of the book by Jean-Marie H.: "I love the newness of original Christianity, that does not demand we exit from human history in order to reply to man's question about himself and God. It is within this history that we hear this Gospel word, so full of mysterious and marvelous trust: 'Whoever loves God, knows God.'"

If only the God "in question" were really expressing himself in these words! I listen out for him.

Here, Saint Benedict and every one of us (whether nun or monk) intervenes here and there in history.

LISTEN.

"Come to me. I will give you rest.
Learn from me, for I am meek and humble of *heart*."

[07/15/1994] The 15th.

To hear myself rehearse my tiresome and unseemly violence again this morning, sends me far away from the community, excludes me radically from this protected place. One question has shaken me: Should I join the violent? No, nothing attracts me to their battle; but do I truly belong among those people, as that brother said to me who was incensed by my violence and convinced that he was completely free of it? Difficult to preside at the Eucharist in this state of mind. I haven't been able to free myself of this bad humor in me. "A mortal illness," the king said. Will my bitter bitterness lead me to PEACE?

Suzanne on the phone: a feminine voice. She did not seem to be too afraid . . . of me, bad monk! I couldn't have a proper conversation with her.

[07/16/1994] July 16th.

Feast day back in Ancône. "But if I lack love . . ."

[07/17/1994] July 17th.

A Sunday apart
it is here [. . .]

[07/18/1994] Monday.

[07/22/1994] Friday.

Before Lauds, Mohammed asks me for hoes to dig up the potatoes. With a great desire for the WORD, I want to remember this, in connection with our work together in the gardens: "You know: it's as if the same blood runs through us, irrigates us together."

Thus, for him, blood speaks first of all of LIFE, of a shared, common life.

[07/24/1994] Sunday 24th.

Went off into the mountains, all alone.

[07/25/1994] The 25th.

Saint Christopher (and Saint James, apostle and martyr). We shall drink your cup, we are drinking it.

[07/27/1994] The 27th.

Never despair. You are not a mirage, a deceitful brook.
There is in my life   right here   a treasure   a pearl.

[07/29/1994] Friday.

The saints of Bethany, Martha, Mary and Lazarus   whom he awakened from the dead.

Then the high priests decided to kill Lazarus too
since many of the Jews were going away because of him
and put their faith in Jesus.

Across from us the forest is burning. And I am distressed about our well! Yesterday Rabah brought me these words from his son Amin (it was his elder brother's day of circumcision):

"And what about my friend Christophe? We must give him a piece of cake . . ."

The best part is received here, in our simple and basic daily life.

[08/04/1994] Thursday, August 4th.

Saint John-Mary Vianney, the Curé of Ars. I am resting. In solitude, too. And I should like to be at prayer. Five French persons murdered in Algiers yesterday. People are talking about it, and that's exactly what their murderers were looking for. The terrorists have something to say that the authorities do not want to hear. It's the repressed and choked word that explodes in a fury and madness that kill. Nevertheless, I accept with open arms this day offered me. There is fatigue—an invasive lassitude—in the hot air. An image comes to mind: "The Lord is my shepherd. I lack nothing. He makes me rest."

And I hear you say to me: "I am the good shepherd"
It is I. I know my own and my own know me
As the Father knows me and I know the Father
and I forsake my very soul for the sheep.
I give-a-life-for . . .

["to give" here has the meaning of "laying down," "setting before," especially for the sacrificial offering]

A. Chouraqui translates Isaiah 53:12 like this: "because he stripped his being down to the point of death."

You ask me to choose life, but in this choice
there is the event of your death, that brings your life to me
and therefore also your extreme denudation.

Last Sunday I was at the end of my rope. I could have had empathized with my brothers' fatigue, with the despair of the Algerians, muted in their heart. But there was this ego I couldn't get around: exasperated in choir, distressed over the scarcity of water.

I picked up from the wastebasket what I wrote then, to face it and not be completely defeated.

For one thing
It's all about you for whom I have left every place
leaving even friendship behind and I no longer know
today

whether and how
it is still true
I no longer succeed in behaving as a brother
and I've lost the skill of being a child
firmly joined to the one who infinitely
in full liberty
loves us
well
in choir, we go flat the office is so heavy it makes
me sick
and I feel after Lauds on this Day of the Lord
like a clot of bad blood obstructing the fountainhead
and blocking all possibility of a happy offering

it is there
ah if you could lay your hand
touch me with yourself
but you who are to blame for this messy existence
will you tell me where
I really am?

in your madness
you have cast me here I cling and persist in believing
in this burning trajectory which today still
has me in its sights
right here
where nothing can take my place
and if I stay
it's as one released from all vows
one interiorly abandoned even while exteriorly
the ocso form still subsists[41]

your friend is sick and I have a hunch already
in their eyes I sense Evil

41. "OCSO" stands for "Order of Cistercians of the Strict Observance," to which Christophe Lebreton belonged. Members of the Order sometimes pronounce this acronym *oxo*, as if it were a word. At this time Brother Christophe seems to be interiorly wrenched, so that he is experiencing a dichotomy between his subjective and his official identity.

I stay   to see
you put it well   you blessed you pure   you will see

P.S. The mail hardly ever arrives here any more, the bridge
has been blown up
the forest is burning   there is no water
and it is hot
and then here you know
killing happens here a lot

a glance at history shows that failure obviously dominates
unless from your cross
your hand
writes
in us
in me too
illegible love

Did I have to transcribe these words, uttered secretly?
It's done. Onward! Let us
recite your poem today
yes you will kiss me today with your mouth
you give your life as the Lover lays down the Kiss in which the whole Gift is fulfilled.

Standing, Mary clings to the Gift: she is so kissed that through her the love reaches all others.[42]

I re-read my notes from Marguerite Porete:

(ch. 5) But there is another life that we call "the peace of charity in an annihilated life," p. 66 [God loves in me what surpasses me: no longer what exceeds me by being in him]; p. 85: What surpasses her is what inebriates her, and it will never be otherwise.

42. "She is so kissed that through her the love reaches all others": This is one possible rendering of the very elliptical and original phrase: *embrassée vers tous trans-aimée.*

(ch. 24) In the true liberty of pure Love: thus they do nothing that is against the peace of their interior state, and they thus bear in peace whatever Love disposes (*cf.* ch. 29).

(ch. 31) Calm down! Your will is enough for your beloved. He will love nothing without you, nor will you love anything without him.

(ch. 36) By his courtesy, he has established me in such a way that he wants what I want and he wants nothing that I do not want. And I am in peace. The reason is that we have this agreement, he and I. For your courtesy and nobility desire that I also should be in peace because you are in peace. This is so much so, Lord, that I see that you have acquitted yourself well of this debt—which was to give me peace—for whatever I encounter, whatever happens or might have happened with my sins, your peace is always left me.

Where is this soul, then? Where she loves, without feeling it.

(ch. 42) This knowing-nothing and this wanting-nothing give her everything, and allow her to find the buried and hidden treasure, contained eternally in the Trinity.

(ch. 45) People who have no will live in the liberty of charity [knowing their nothingness]. They have come to trust what is beyond them, and the knowledge that is born of this trust consists precisely in knowing nothing about it (p. 117). This excess of peace in which she lives, perdures, is and will be without her proper being. [. . .] She abides and is transformed into what is beyond her by this excess of eternal weight, although she is found nowhere: she loves in that sweet country called Excess of Peace. He has given me peace, and I live only on the peace that is born of his gifts in my soul, without any thought; and thus I am nothing if this is not given me: here is my all, and what I have that is the best in me.

(ch. 53) Who are the people of the mountain? [!!!][43] They are those who have nothing on earth, neither shame, nor honor, nor fear of anything that might happen to them.

43. Porete's phrase "the people of the mountain," in her context referring to those who are searching for God, draws a chuckle from Brother Christophe because it is the local Algerian nickname for the terrorist rebels.

An opening that opens like lightning, closes immediately and one cannot remain there for long . . . the peace given in this opening . . . the alternating operation of Far-and-Near that enraptures her . . . no one would believe what extremity of peace [peace upon peace upon peace] this soul receives . . . the sudden appearance of the glory of the soul.

(ch. 66) The divine school is held within her.

(ch. 71) This union of achieved peace reaches me and merges with me.

(ch. 74) Bride of peace . . . the gift of the divine love of unity—and this unity gives her peace and the delicate nourishment of the glorious country where her Beloved dwells. She is no longer nourished by what she possesses, but by her life as a gleaner. This food is that of my chosen bride, who is Mary-of-Peace: she is Mary-of-Peace because Tender Love feeds her.

(ch. 77) Understand, by Love—Love begs you—that Love has so much to give and lays down so few conditions, that in one single moment it unites two things into but one.

Whoever trusts in God is great, strong, most free and unencumbered by all things, for then God sanctifies him. All that one does with oneself is wholly encumbered by the self.

(ch. 81) This soul is detained and imprisoned in the land of complete peace. For she always dwells in complete satisfaction [*cf.* Rule of Saint Benedict, chapter 7, satisfied with everything].

(ch. 85) This soul is free, more than free, perfectly free, simply free, in root and trunk and all its branches and in all the fruit on its branches.

(ch. 86) Mary has but . . . one single intention that allows her to find peace, but Martha is always having new intentions, so that her peace is always disrupted.

(ch. 89) Thus, she never came to know abundant and continual peace until she was purely and wholly stripped of her ability to want.

(ch. 93) The Virgin Mary: to want only the divine will. This is what was, is and will be her divine gaze, her divine nourishment, her divine love, her divine peace, her divine praise, all her work and rest.

(ch. 94) The language of this life, which is the divine life, is the secret silence of divine love. No longer is there any other life here than always wanting the divine will.

(ch. 96) In the name of God, let us never allow anything of ourselves or of others to come into us which would make God exit his goodness.

(ch. 101) From the moment Love opened its book [. . .] this opening has made me see so clearly [. . .], and the light from the opening of this book has made me find what is mine and dwell in it.

(ch. 102) There are no small faults; what does not please the divine will must necessarily displease it.

(ch. 103) See how God has freely given me my free will. He has given me everything, no matter how little my will desires it.

(ch. 106) His demands are foreign to every country. This "other" is secret Love and is beyond all peace, there where my love is anchored without me.

(ch. 117) God has nowhere left to put his Goodness but in me, he has nowhere left to find proper shelter and cannot find where to put all of himself, except in me. P. 209: It's on the basis of [God's] demands that one may go further; it's through demands than one may find one's way and go back to it if one has strayed.

(ch. 133) And this Wanting-Nothing sows the divine seed that is taken from the divine will. This seed can never be lacking but only the few dispose themselves to receive it. Tender Love makes one have but one love and but one will, and that is why all my wanting has become nothing but Wanting-Nothing.

(ch. 136) And you have never existed, dear Father, dear Brother, dear Beloved, for even a single moment without my being thus loved by you.

In the afternoon I read F.X. Durrwell:[44] *Le Christ, l'homme et la mort* ["Christ, Man and Death"]. I meet Brother Henri and Sister

44. François-Xavier Durrwell, CSSR (1912–2005), French Redemptorist and theologian, renowned as the biblical theologian of Christ's paschal mystery.

Paule-Hélène as I turn the pages. "The apostolate of a Christian through his death is likewise incomparable. It fulfills a desire that no activity on earth could satisfy. [. . .] Suddenly, all apostolic possibilities are lifted up to a higher plane and given a coefficient that is still unknown in the total communion with Christ, in his universal redemptive death. The hour then arrives for a charity that makes the limits of self-giving burst open, the hour of a weakness that makes the creature surrender completely to omnipotence, the hour when Christ leads his Spouse into the full sharing of his being and his action.

"When she (the Church) descends into her own depths, and there finds her truth in charity, in prayer and in humble service, and finally in death, then she is joining Christ in his own death and communing in his resurrection and in the cosmic power of the Holy Spirit. (p. 71)

"The Church is Christ's companion in his encounter with men. [. . .] And now the decisive moment has arrived, the last option: here is death! [. . .] May she [the Church] stand in love and prayer, stand by Christ, who wants to save men in their death." (p. 91)

[08/07/1994] 19th Sunday.

At Mass I hear 1 Kings 19:4,[45] and I understand You: the God who asks for too much. You really believe that we are capable of this "too much." This is actually what we believers experience. Written on a board, near the scales (no doubt by M., Mohammed's brother-in-law), I read this: *Why I am always sad?* [*sic*] *I am always sad. Why?* [in English in the original].

[08/15/1994] After August 15th. . .

Qoheleth, for his part, thinks: "There is a time to kill and a time to heal." Everybody is sick of the way murder is infesting

45. "[Elijah] himself went on into the wilderness, a day's journey, and sitting under a furze bush wished that he were dead. 'Lord', he said, 'I have had enough. Take my life; I am no better than my ancestors.' "

our time. And on the cross you open the time for healing. "M strength and my fortress." In you my heart trusts: he has heale me, my flesh blooms anew. What's precisely the truth about m flesh? Lazarus' flesh in the tomb. My friend, will you let me se even more of my own corruption?

Today, I hear in the Gospel that there is a WEDDING: the sor of the king is marrying a lady . . . and everybody is invited.

[08/19/1994] Friday.

Pardon and Peace from you, in the Breath: this comes to me at the foot of the Cross. Yesterday morning, in Medea, twelve bodies were thrown into the street for everybody to see; massacred, mutilated. . . . That is the answer from the forces of law and order to those on the other side, after an attack on a police officer whose throat was cut in a shop near the market. Near the Cross.

[8/20/1994] The 20th.

Saint Bernard and *Mulud*.[46] Last night, chapter with our father the bishop. He resembles you, carrying his pastoral burden: a servant of the Gospel in this time of violence. It is good for us to receive him and love him.

At Vigils, Psalm 8 speaks to me: "Your splendor is sung up to the heavens by the mouth of children and of babes: this is a bulwark you set up against the adversary, where the enemy is shattered in his revolt."

On his return from Medea and still shocked by what he had seen, Mohammed said to me: "The worst thing is that Muslims did this to Muslims. It's terrible." In Rwanda, Christians did it to Christians. Indeed, the faith is being tested, shaken.

I can't bring myself truly to join M., the son of Ali, in his stubborn and indefatigable praise: *alhamdulillah*.[47] His praise is

46. *Mulud* is the Arabic name of the prophet Mohammed's birthday, celebrated on the 12th day of the Islamic month of Rabi' al-Awwal.

47. *Alhamdulillah*: "Praise be to Allah."

pure, surely, but it seems to me it is also combined with an immense sadness, pent-up and hidden, the sadness of suppressed revolt, of impotence. I remember D.V.'s "analysis" [. . .], pointing to a deep-seated ambiguity in the "Muslim" conscience. Moussa isn't far from recognizing it himself, for several times he has said to me: "You know, in our heart there are good things and then again bad things also." Yesterday, he made me a gesture of peace after a misunderstanding in our shared life. Ben Aissa touches me deeply too: he seems happy in the relationship he has with us here, whereas before he no doubt had only a limited view.

[08/21/1994] Sunday.

"And you, do you want to go away?"

To go away. Jesus knows what it is: to go against the Father who gives us to Him, to go against the Gift that draws me to You, and in You I go to the Father.

"To whom would we go?" To be here in order to go to you. This is beyond a choice between different possibilities. We are not at the convergence of different roads, but before you, who are the Way that opens out. And I am caught up in the event: drawn by your freedom as Son as if by your inhaling breath.

To believe becomes the only locomotion that is worthwhile: going to You. A way that is almost obligatory but that does no violence at all to myself and invites me to keep on moving on that path,

precisely on this way where your hand leads me
a way opens up and at the same "time"
an impulse runs through me   I can back down
or consent.

[08/26/1994] Friday 26th.

The day before yesterday, and yesterday also, military men spent the night at the school. This morning I meet Mohammed, his face downcast, still very upset because he saw them arrive while he was watering his garden. It's getting closer, they say.

And we are celebrating Mariam, the "little" Arab girl: she knew how to speak the language of the Cross. She kept watch and the Bridegroom arrived. Christian takes the plane tomorrow.

You set the table for me before my enemies. For the only attitude that resists Evil, that stands firm against its decision to kill, is the Gift.

[08/27/1994] Saint Monica.

When Christian was leaving, he said to me: Look after them well! And you too, look after yourself. Yes, it's a pastoral obligation.

[09/01/1994] Thursday, September 1st.

"Go forward into deep water and pay out your nets."

Such going out derives from a singular act of foolish obedience. Then one participates in a collective effort: fishing together.

The deep water is the Relationship to you. The abyss of my misery is saved. The deep water where everything is grace draws me toward a mysterious elevation.

[09/02/1994] Friday.

The whole of your promise is pure, and I may hope that it can make me pure also, by you, in you, with you.

[09/04/1994] Sunday.

Open yourself up. This Opening-up is something that can only be received, received from another whose whole being touches me, awakening desire. A week ago I heard the voices of my mother, then of my father on the phone. Jesus opens me up still further: to infinity. Don't fail to be present to the Opening, where the Gift rushes in and draws me in its breath all the way to the † where You, Jesus, keep life open.

[09/07/1994] Wednesday.

A "deviant Transcendence," says an editorial in *La Croix* about the Islamists. "God is greater," chants the muezzin.

Is it possible to be a stumbling block to a brother, something that will make him fall? May my sin not be the only cause of this scandal that tests both of us.

[09/09/1994] Friday.

While I keep watch in the vineyard, I am finishing Karl Stern's *The Burning Bush*.[48] I am captivated by this truthful book. P. 319: "I knew in the depth of my being there and then that we have to commune in the body and blood of Christ, whether with our persecutors or our friends. That is the true, lasting and only remedy for hate."

P. 323: "There is an extraordinary side to the suffering of Christ. It seems to include all human suffering and yet can be completed by the suffering of separate individuals. It contains all human suffering."

P. 325-6: "We cannot forget that it is Christ himself who is present in so many sufferings. It was he and his mother. . . ."

"There is enough Evil in me to last me a lifetime of fighting against it. But the Gospel asks for our immediate intervention, now, at this moment, and in the place where we find ourselves. It says that our soul, with the aid of Grace, contains enough energy to change the world."

[09/12/1994] 09/12.

Saint Peter of Tarentaise.[49] Twenty years ago (!) I was getting ready to leave my home (in Coulanges) to go to Albertville and

48. Karl Stern (1906–1975), German-Canadian psychiatrist, neuroscientist, and writer, convert from Orthodox Judaism to the Catholic Church.

49. Saint Peter of Tarentaise (1102–1174), founder and first abbot of the Abbey of Tamié in Haute-Savoie, the home monastery of Brother Christophe Lebreton. Abbot Peter was later appointed archbishop of Tarentaise, modern-day Moûtiers, in the Rhône-Alpes region of southeastern France.

enter Tamié. "Who can keep God from showing me mercy?" (Raïssa Maritain[50])

[09/15/1994] Thursday.

Yom Kippur. Peace through the blood of the Cross. Tuesday: one of their visits. Three of them, plus another wounded one who was brought on a donkey. Brother Luc receives them as if they were You. Everyone around us notices. In the evening it's the army's turn.

Today—Our Lady of Sorrows.

A letter from Jean-Bernard and Didier. Mom has given us a mission to fulfill: to offer up our lives that the world may be saved, that the Lord may do his will in the three of us, through Mom's hands. . . .

[09/16/1994] The 16th.

Saint Cyprian. Unless the grain does not fall into the earth—delivered into this earth that is held in your HAND—and does not die . . . Sacrament of Reconciliation. I love what Jean-Pierre said to me on the basis of John: an irruption of Light: it does not come to obliterate or confound all my darkness but to illuminate it so that the Light may burst up within it.

[09/21/1994] The 21st.

About Tamié: I remember having left there. This distance indwells me.

Moussa and I are talking in the garden. I'd forgotten to turn off a tap. I say: "There's only one thing we mustn't forget." Moussa says: "Yes, but still, there are other things that are important too . . . , for instance, if you forget to help someone you'd started to help, if you forget to keep a promise. . . ." And we agree in

50. Raïssa Maritain (1883–1960), Russian Jewish convert to the Catholic Church, spiritual writer, and poet, wife of the renowned Catholic philosopher Jacques Maritain.

recognizing that these important things are the sign that our memory of God is not a lie, an illusion that masks our selfishness.

[09/22/1994] The 22nd.

Voting in the community is a beautiful thing—an occasion that is welcoming, open, without weakness, discerning, benevolent. It's a very pure experience: Your will at the heart of our (consecrated) poverty. It's also an experience of fruitful chastity: no fidgeting about a desire to have a child (or children) at no matter what price, but the consciousness of a maternal responsibility (a responsibility "out of the womb," as A. Chouraqui would put it).

[09/23/1994] The 23rd.

Mary at the foot of the Cross is giving birth. It is time to be born: to go off to the Eternal, who is nothing but *I love you*.

[09/26/1994] The 26th.

In the scriptorium just now, after Vigils, while reading Deuteronomy, I began to write: "Following God." On top of that I added "It's been about," and then still further up "For twenty years," as if it were a title of something! For twenty years / it's been about / following God. What is most palpable is this enduring quality, inspired by the Eternal. Today I have a hunch that even more is involved. Three days with the Poor Clares will help me better to understand your Grace and your Desire. Whatever follows will come from you being lifted up, from you drawing me toward your *I am*. What are you asking for?

As for You: Do keep every word, do fill up the whole space and do recognize me as your beloved.

[09/27/1994] The 27th.

The question that probes me, that intrigues me, is: "Why do I go on?" What concerns me is your future in me, in us. . . .

[10/01/1994] October 1st.

Yesterday I came back from Algiers with Gilles and Robert after two and a half days with the Poor Clares, and on Friday the meeting with the priests of the archdiocese. After supper they were there. I tried to dissuade and restrain P., who was brandishing a gospel in which I couldn't recognize you. There is no ready-made answer that's the right one. The existential answer is to be found in a Faith that is naked and poor. Even more so because their intentions (that night) were manifestly not belligerent in our regard. We risk taking sides, if not becoming actually divided, on this point; but we don't yet seem inclined to get to know them, to listen to them, to join them in what they are, without betraying what we profess to be: Christian monks. In my own mind I'll have to go over again what I did not succeed in expressing properly (it's a bit humiliating!) at the priests' meeting about Father Sanson's opinions. A simple presentation, intelligible to reason, would undoubtedly be useful to make us step back and face the situation more clearly. But the forces now at work make such a rationale always seem to me to come too late, and it is therefore ineffective and useless for the actors in the drama. It seems to be a matter of an inter-Islamic war. Why do we stay here? To count the blows and make forecasts? What's happening here is not only "Muslim," and what is going on in Bosnia-Serbia and in Rwanda is not only "Christian."

[10/02/1994] Sunday.

And I believe in You. Your faith goes right through me, and I go to God.

Nothing ought to make one deviate from this principle of principles: the Gospel is possessed truth only insofar as it is a joyous gift of life, and this life is love, and this love is lived and enjoyed right here among us. (p. 39, *Incipit*, by M. Bellet[51]). The dreadful things to which the Gospel gives witness are the mark

51. Maurice Bellet, *Incipit ou le commencement* (Paris: Desclée de Brouwer, 1996).

left on this love by the atrociousness that haunts mankind. Because this love, colliding with the sadness and cruelty in which we find ourselves, gives rise to a great conflict—and it can only be expressed in extreme images. But woe if this violence in the Gospel is perceived from a position of fear and resentment! [. . .] P. 41: We must keep on going back to the beginning, whose presence is found in what we actually are to each other. The road that I speak of is not a mere dream. Whoever goes forward on that road will arouse around him all the murderous powers and all the sadness in the world. Not a touch here of utopian affectation. That wayfarer will go right through the middle of it—which means he will be bruised, crushed, without turning aside, not letting himself be contaminated and entrapped by the spirit of destruction, to the very end: to speak, to care, to give, to love—nothing is left out, no one is left out.

The true beginning of man, the point without support, appears like lightning at the heart of what is murky and distressful.

[10/06/1994] The 6th.

Yesterday morning Moussa said, while he was sowing beans: "There's only one in all of Algeria who doesn't try to grab POWER: GOD. What he's searching for is the Good of man." Then he returns to a conviction that he has often shared with me and that we can discuss: evil, bad things, are in the heart of each of us. I hear you saying it, you who know what is in the heart of man.

[10/07/1994] October 7th.

Our Lady of the Rosary. Mary praying. Was it in '87 or in '88? I was coming back to Algeria. Keep me here in your (crucified) truth. Keep us in your *I love you*: as disciples.

[10/09/1994] Sunday.

Exchange in the garden yesterday. Moussa: "In your opinion, do you put out fire with water or with gasoline?" Me: "With water." M.: "Good! And, you know . . . here there's one only who's not trying to grab power. It's Him: God." Me: "What he wants is our happiness." Moussa: "Yes. Our good. But it's Money that rules now. Our country is under God's protection. But everybody's afraid." Then we talk about violence and of the power that is stronger and doesn't seek to dominate. In the evening I hear of the murder of a Frenchman in Algiers and of the massacre in Switzerland of 54 people belonging to a sect. Our humanity is under a death threat. Jesus reminds us of the commandments. "Thou shalt not kill" [in Arabic in the text: *la taqtul*].

You need only one thing. To Martha you said: your duty is only one, only one thing is necessary. It is to choose the part Mary chose (Marc Lacan[52]): to follow You. You who look at me and love me. Gamble your life on that "yes," so that your life may be 'yes' to the presence that urges the gamble and expects it (M. Lacan). To follow you is to enter into your Pasch, to venture forth into the Opening. To follow God, to walk in your Presence. To cling to the Gift.

A matter of conscience, they say.

We are considered accomplices for not having opposed (violently!) the demand on the phone. We are accomplices anyway—in solidarity with others in the Evil that has not yet been dislodged from us. I am an accomplice: violence has not been uprooted from my heart. I am not yet disarmed. And so, I'm an accomplice. Just the same, I am not going to let myself be locked into this abstract problem—always dwarfed by events and so useless in helping us face it as we should. Isn't the truth of the matter that we're trying to find our own justice, our own moral purity? What's the good of being faithful to an image? I am learning something else: to become an accomplice of the Innocent. And to receive from Him the attitude, the gesture, and even the words, adjusted as all these are to the precise measure of our listening ability, of our availability, of our obedience. I am learning freedom in the SPIRIT. He is the DEFENDER.

52. Marc-François Lacan (1908–1994), Benedictine monk and author of books such as *Dieu n'est pas un assureur* ["God Is Not an Insurer"] and *La Vérité ne s'épuise pas* ["Truth Is Never Exhausted"]. He was the younger brother of the eminent psychoanalyst Jacques Lacan.

[10/10/1994] Monday 10th.

Silouan, I pray to you who are so close to Mary in the communion of saints. Yesterday, when I received the Cup, I felt how much that gesture compromised me: to drink the Blood of non-violence. I still cling so much to the murderous forces within me. Yes, Silouan, I want to look at you and flee from all despair. "But the Holy Spirit teaches us to LOVE; and then we will have compassion even for the demons. They have lost humility and love for God."

A letter from X., who is back-pedaling.

[11/10/1994] The 11th.

I receive the Gospel as a birthday present: a light to my feet. It is about time to start walking straight when you are 44 years old. (Tuesday's texts!) It's in Lk 11:42-46. The great misfortune is to bypass justice [in Arabic in the text: *al-'adl*] and the love of God [in Arabic in the text: *mahhaba Allah*]. Yes, to pass right by them, and one passes very near indeed since the days when your Son, Father, came to walk with us. I beg you to keep me close to his Cross, in the Church, with Mary and all the saints. Open to the Spirit. May it please you for the Spirit to bring forth from me, from us, the fruit of the Tree: love, joy, peace, patience, goodness, goodwill, faith, humility, self-control: resemblance to you according to your grace.

Today I feel the benevolent friendship of Silouan and of Father Pierre, and I am sure that they are friends in You in the joy of the Spirit: praying together for the world, this world so threatened by violent death: Haiti, Serbia, Iraq, AIDS, Algeria (in Algiers a Frenchman, and in Medea a French-speaking female teacher, both with their throats cut).

To drink the blood of the Lamb places us in one camp: that of the victims. Your victory, Jesus, is not easy, in me, in us. I am sure, Love: you win. I should love to take part in the prize of your Victory. I am still so very stingy. Make me understand the GIFT; let it become in me prayer and tears.

Our young neighbor, Ben Yussef Zubir, died yesterday. An army truck hit the car he was in. An innocent victim joined to you, our paschal Lamb. One would like to intervene, to stand in the breach and try to stop this daily massacre. It must be done by a truer, more total form of engagement in prayer.

On the phone, I hear Claire's and Sophie's voices. When Father Amédée says to him *Rubbi maak* ["My God be with you!"], Moussa answers: "Yes, but it must not be only words, you have to mean it here, in the heart."

[10/13/1994] Thursday.

A dream last night: I was alone, lying in the grass in a field, dreaming. A wolf-hound approaches, rather startling but not threatening. I can touch him and make him my companion.

Lk 12:48: "You also testify . . ." Witnesses to murder: ". . . from the blood of Abel to the blood of Zachary" to the blood of Ben Yussef who will not come to surprise me in the garden today, elegantly casual, independent and no doubt a little adrift, except in his search for friendship and truth. We'll no longer practice Arabic dialect together. "You," his father had said to him, "you aren't like us, you love foreigners. But make sure it isn't out of self-interest."

[10/15/1994] Saturday evening.

"Who can live with his truth? But it is enough to know that it is there, it is enough to know it, so that it may nourish in oneself a secret and silent fervor in the face of death." A. Camus,[53] *Le premier homme* ["The First Man"], p. 304. Am re-reading Christian Bobin: "Intelligence is the solitary force that can distil a handful of light from the chaos of one's own life, enough to light the way a little beyond oneself—toward those others out there who, like

53. Albert Camus (1913–1960), the Algerian-French author, journalist, and philosopher who was awarded the Nobel Prize in Literature and is sometimes associated with the Existentialist school.

us, have lost their way in the dark." *L'inespérée* ["The Unexpected"], pp. 28–29.

[10/16/1994] Sunday.

And p. 38: "It's not ink that makes the writing, it's the voice, the voice's solitary truth, the hemorrhage of truth in the womb of the voice. Any person is a writer who follows nothing but the truth of who he is, without ever leaning against anything other than the misery and the solitude of that truth."

[10/17/1994] Saint Luke.

At the end of our feast-day meal, Brother Luc speaks up: "I want to thank Christophe for Chopin, Brother Michael for the good food, W. for the cake and the good wine, Brother Christian for the way he leads the community, and I bet there'll be a crowd around this table in a few years. . . . I think they'll be listening to Bach."

[10/19/1994] The 19th.

A crowd around this table . . . I'm not sure. But I'm sure there will be a great crowd around that other table for the Feast of all the saints. Ben Yussef has gone before us to that meal of FRIENDS. He's gone right through the middle of my existence. I wasn't attached to him (he wouldn't have allowed it). I was moved by the relationship between us, which came about in a carefree way but with intensity, truth, humor and freedom. I'm awaiting our next meeting now, since we parted with a casual "See you tomorrow, *insh' Allah*." The next day was a Friday.

[10/24/1994] Monday 10/24.

At Bab el-Oued, at the church door, at the time of the Eucharist they had celebrated with literal truth, two Spanish sisters were murdered.

[10/26/1994] Wednesday.

Today You invite me to fight. "Make an effort to fight" [in Arabic in the text: *ijtahidû*]. So as to enter through the narrow gate. You open a passage before me. You have grasped my hand. Living consists barely in the time of entering a threshold—which takes a little while—and this suddenly leads into the Inward Country. That happened last Sunday to our two sisters. They won. They crossed the threshold. And are waiting for us on the other side.

Death is a narrow thing: a tightening of the whole of existence in order to move toward an impossible beyond. It's narrow, but it is a door. And that is the sign you gave me—You, the Door—when I came back here (with Mohammed opening one door, and then another, in front of the tractor).

[10/27/1994] Thursday.

Eighth anniversary of the World Day of Prayer in Assisi. Today, Jesus comes up against Herod's homicidal will, and goes his way (Lk 13:31-33). "Finally, arm yourselves with strength from the Lord and from his mighty power," which is nothing but Love (Eph 6).

[10/28/1994] Friday.

Last night, in a dream, I went all the way to Paris to visit Christian's mother. For what reason?

After Vigils, I read the account of your Passion—which is happening to us. I am drawn to this spot where your Cross is raised: a little group of believers standing about you has formed, emerging from you and from your Breath, ushering in "the age of faith." I read again the homily of our bishop at the funeral of the Sisters Esther and Caridad. It moves me and speaks to me, in a very particular and precise way: . . . to receive the message that Esther's and Caridad's LIFE sends us (Esther and I were almost the same age, only a year apart!) . . . the reason why they had chosen to return to Algeria. . . . This is aimed directly at our vocation. . . .

this vocation to an encounter, a service, a communion of values and cultures,

it's part of the future of Algeria,

it's also part of the future of the faith

[and the link to Saint Augustine, that great teacher . . .]

[10/30/1994] Sunday.

Listen, Church: I am.

Listen, I in you, like the Father and me. He in me and I in Him, we are ONE.

Listen: I am in you the Resurrection: the LIFE.

Thanks to You (in You, with You), I break through the wall. There is my sin standing before me—this lack of love—given to my brothers—thanks to you, I don't remain—not for very long—frightened, in despair. . . .

I break through death. When will my existence as a brother be lived on that other side, for you want to see us arrive together at this eternal LIFE.

Today you say to me: get up, go toward yourself, toward your paschal Self.

This afternoon Mohammed is inviting Christian and me to have coffee at his house. He's just finished laying down the floor in the entrance and the bedroom. The future of faith comes to meet us in this shared story.

[11/01/1994] 01/11.

ALL SAINTS. And the anniversary of the independence of the country. Onward, you humiliated ones who belong to the Spirit; the kingdom of heaven is yours. Onward, you peacemakers; you shall be shouted 'sons of Elohim'. In 1980: the day of my Profession at Tamié: a shout proclaims us beloved, the race of God's children.

[11/06/1994] Sunday.

The jar of flour shall not go empty, or the jug of oil run dry.[54] That is elementary existence: living does not happen by itself. (Jean-François Marquet was found at Bouira, his throat cut.) Living is an act of faith that stems from a lack. Without You I falter, I perish, I fall. Be my support, my shelter in distress, make me live.

From her need that woman contributed all she had, her whole livelihood.[55]

The monastic community at Fez has its origin in this Gospel passage.

Saint Bernard, *Sermon on the Song of Songs* (61, 7 and 8). The pale gold of Jesus crucified and the pallor of the Church, the dove in the clefts of the rock. "All her affections are preoccupied with the wounds of Christ, and she abides in them by constant meditation. From this comes her endurance for martyrdom and her immense trust in the Most High. The martyr [Paule-Hélène, Henri, Caridad, Esther] need not be afraid of raising his bloodless and bruised face to him by whose deathly pallor he is healed: to present to him a glorious likeness of his death, even in the paleness of gold. Why should he fear, since the Lord himself says to him: 'Show me your face. [. . .] God wants to be seen, not to see. [. . .] From the rock comes the courage of the martyr, from it his power to drink the Lord's cup, for the joy of the Lord is our strength."

Tanguy,[56] I think of you as I re-read Christian Bobin: "A painter is someone who cleans the windowpane between the world and us with light, with a cloth of light saturated with silence" (*L'inespérée*, p. 72).

54. *Cf.* 1 Kings 17:7-14.
55. *Cf.* Mark 12:44.
56. Yves Tanguy (1900–1955), French surrealist painter.

[11/08/1994] Tuesday.

Yesterday we were sowing (oats and green peas for fodder). At chapter in the evening, we discussed the appeal from the bishops to form small groups in times of trial. Who is available? I re-read Ruth's promise to Naomi, and I would love to be able to live it in truth, in poverty: "Wherever you go, I will go. Wherever you live, I will live. Your people shall be my people, and your God, my God."

To follow God: here.

[11/12/1994] Saturday 12/11.

Three persons, heavily armed, seen by the doctor last night.

Cardinal Decourtray:[57] "There are certain kinds of panic that do not harmonize well with the indwelling in us of the Holy Trinity."

Something from You—the Gift given to your friends—has met them and taken care of them.

But it was also You who came as a sick man to meet the truest part of these artisans of death. Yes, they are sick at heart, inhabited by a fratricidal violence. But what is the truth of my own heart? The killers resort to the doctor. There is a time to kill and a time to heal, says Qoheleth. Brother Luc's battle: he's a doctor who prays. May each of us be like that in what he has been given to do: in the workshop, in the kitchen, in the garden: workers who pray.

[11/15/1994] Tuesday 15.

"'What shall we do?' Elisha answered: 'Do not be afraid, our side outnumbers theirs.' And Elisha prayed thus: 'Lord, open his eyes, that he may see.' And the Lord opened the eyes of the servant, so that he saw the mountainside filled with horses and fiery chariots around Elisha" (2 Kings 6:15-17).

57. Albert Cardinal Decourtray (1923–1994), Archbishop of Lyons, engaged in inter-religious dialogue, especially with the Jews.

Those people, M. says to me, will not win. It's impossible: they've done too much harm to the people.

It's a very stripped-down Faith, very poor, very beautiful, threatened but nevertheless finding something solid, stronger than hatred: they will not win.

Love: on the cross, You win. There are many who gather around you.

30 deaths in Berrouaghia. This information is circulating around the monastery.

[11/16/1994] Wednesday.

How strange, the reaction of W., who's been in Algiers since Sunday: "People are free in these streets. Life is being lived. Is real life to be found other than in the cloister?" Good question. It also expresses a need for relaxation to ease the pressure.

[11/24/1994] Thursday 24th.

Three more came for treatment yesterday. Very polite. "Friendly faces," W. tells me, who received them. Christian our prior returns tonight, *insh' Allah.* To obey is honorable only if the authority to whom you submit is free. God entrusts the exercise of his infinitely free power to Jesus, his Envoy. Jesus is my king when my life is caught up in this undertaking: all power over my flesh. The Eucharist is a place where this reign is experienced as liberating.

[11/26/1994] Saturday, 11/26. Advent.

To finish this liturgical year (well), I ask and receive the grace of FORGIVENESS. You put me back on my feet to walk, to run, upright, toward you who are coming.

> He comes
> and every eye shall see him.

He comes: his FACE, and that is infinitely everything

To say to you "come" is irreconcilable with a flight from the world
which would be something other than coming
and living on this covenanted earth.

Detached, to come to this world, to the point of giving him my life.

The monastic enclosure in Algeria has no reason to subsist as an abstract category. Its perimeter can be moved . . . as a security measure.

But then it will no longer exist

It signifies that You are coming here to save us.

A letter from M.-F.: "It seems to me that this 'confrontation' has made us take a big step forward in the truth, toward what is really the deep heart of each one of us. And it is irreversible. So much the better!"

Hadewijch:[58] "As soon as I understood in highest fidelity / that Love would help me at all times, no alien suffering afflicted me / I remained upright in trust / knowing that one day / Love would give me the kiss of union."

May I say to you "come," as long as you want me to remain here.

[11/28/1994] 11/28.

Yes, this stabilizes me into a single desire (so many others fight against it, including the desire to be finished with it all).

To live at Tibhirine—to dwell in your gardens: with reference to You who are coming.

[12/01/1994] December 1st.

Bashir says: "Brother Henri's someone we shouldn't forget."

2nd Sunday of Advent. We are on retreat since last evening, guided by Father Gabriel Piroird, our neighboring bishop from

58. Hadewijch, 13th-century poet and mystic, probably from the Duchy of Brabant in the Netherlands.

Constantine. God in the image of man: What image of God is in me, and how did it take shape? My reflection is like an adventure that draws me toward the unknown. You, beyond any mental image. I find in myself something like impressions of you that were left and stay there, strong and tenacious. I remember the little boy I was, walking beside my friendly Granpa, greeting everyone as he passed: an impression of You walking and greeting everybody, and me happy to be with You like a child.

I remember Granma too: she was gravely ill, and I ask You to let me take her place. In the face of suffering I feel you are near, concerned, and I have the impression that I can do something. Is this, then, the image of a god who demands a death (mine)? There is certainly something of that, twisting the true desire to do something to let Granma live, because I cannot accept her death. A desire to make a vital offering. From my large family, from my Mom and Dad, I received a Christian conscience, the possibility of growing up in this tradition, which is all at once Catholic and French and middle-class and rural. And in the middle of it all, an unspoken suffering. You are also there when we do night prayers around the bed, and when we celebrate You on Sunday as one united and well-dressed family, with our place reserved in the village church. One day I see another house: the minor seminary. The idea comes to me to go there, and this has everything to do with You who call us to leave everything and invite us to make up our minds.

Mesmon S'Ha is the victim of an attack. A French *pied-noir*[59] has been killed in Oran. ✝ All that happens here in Algeria and on earth is simply added to the "idea" of God as belonging to "my house, my tribe, my coterie."

From La Vrillière I went to the minor seminary: same structure of belonging and coherence. Maybe that's where I shut you in and also make myself there a prisoner of a happiness that is real but a little over-protected and enclosed. I get an image of goodness from Father Bodard. There's a real openness with the

59. *Pied-noir* ["black-foot"]: Person of (usually) French origin who lived in Algeria before Algerian independence.

new team and Father Sandrin. It's my decisive year of philosophy, with Michèle Reboul and (poetic) writing. There is also that special woman: my mystical outlook, which partially idealizes our encounter, makes the whole thing made impossible. May 1968[60] permanently destabilizes any idea of institution as such. I desert the ecclesial cocoon. You remain in me as the Forgotten One, sometimes as the Disowned One. I have betrayed your Love. Is there guilt? A difficult responsibility: lack of ambition and confidence in myself and in society. No one is any longer calling me to be, to live, to grow. What remains in me is a religious sense. For instance, when I read the Bhagavad Gita. With Emmaus and the youth camps. There is Abbé Pierre[61] as prophet. What he says about God speaks to me and motivates my "secular" commitment to serve those who suffer most, and to fight for a just world. I feel the urgency of harmonizing my existence with this "commitment," which gradually is becoming more central in my life. Friendship with Philippe G., on his way to Kabul. My relationship with J.: and here it's as if the image of God were being hindered, repressed: I am a victim of my inhibitions, which greatly hamper the growth of a love relationship. If I had acknowledged You at that time, I should have been more of a true man. Dissatisfaction. Sadness. Disgust with myself. God: deliberately you. Unclean for The Word. And that's the experience—in Tours, in my student room, watching for . . . not an image of God. But there was this *I love you* tearing at my flesh: an act of bewildered trust. The recognition of Someone, an Other, there, between Bernadette and me. Someone concretely absent that for

60. "May 1968": The beginning of a volatile period of civil unrest in France. The events began with a series of student occupation protests, followed by strikes involving as many as 11,000,000 workers. These events had a resounding impact on French society that would be felt for decades to come.

61. Abbé Pierre (born Henri Grouès, 1912–2007): French Catholic priest, member of the Resistance during World War II, and former deputy to parliament from the Popular Republican Movement (MRP). In 1949, he founded the *Chiffoniers d'Emmaus* ["Rag-pickers of Emmaus"], with the goal of helping poor and homeless people and refugees.

a moment saves me, rescues me, enacting from within that *I love you* which is said, proclaimed, as if I were looking at Him.

This has continued until today, and it places me squarely before You in this *I love you* whose reality teaches me how difficult it is to live in truth.

All that will follow—it is Jesus who will fashion it in me through the Gift. It's a matter of obedience. Is the image of God here now? What there is, is a desire to see, and life as a purification of sight. In my flesh: TO SEE YOU.

All these ideas-images-impressions of GOD make me the subject of a cultural and religious tradition. At the same time, it seems to me that I am evolving toward enrolling myself in all freedom within "my" Christian tradition. This freedom is born from a living relationship with You, Christ Jesus, my Lord and my God: it springs from the locus of Revelation and Redemption: the CROSS, still very much raised today on our bruised earth. Mary believed outside all religion. She was no longer a Jew at the foot of the Cross—nor a Roman Catholic Christian either.

Facing death, tell me—Love—that my faith will be steadfast. Suddenly, I am terrified of believing.

[12/05/1994] Monday.

From the Book of Tobit. Sarah prays at an open window. Saïd Mekbel[62] (Mesmon S'Ha) has died. He has surely joined those "two women who went to God to ask for grace." He is interceding along with Esther and Caridad so that the balance will tip toward peace and Mercy. Saïd is suddenly so close. Your dream of light has become reality.

62. Saïd Mekbel (1940–1994), well-known Algerian journalist, editor-in-chief of a French-language daily.

[12/06/1994] Tuesday.

Tobias heals his father Tobit. To be a son is just that. Being a father is simply to see your son: "I see you, my son!"[63] Do I let myself be seen, looked at? 'You are my son, Christophe!' At bottom, my lack of self-confidence nourishes my fears and my violence, and that lack comes from not being present to the Gaze that gives birth to me: you want my joy, you want me to live a free and happy life in the Gift.

I must believe that You love to look at who I am becoming. I must believe your eyes: the nakedness of your *I love you*, that strips me naked. Just like Jesus on the cross: surrendered to your gaze, alone and trusting desperately. Certain he's being sought, certain he's being found even in this wretched place of perdition.

[12/07/1994] 7/12.

At First Vespers of the Immaculate Conception, a new (Kabylan) altar: from the chapel of the Little Sisters at Bab el-Oued that they had to leave behind. Around this very altar Esther, Caridad, Henri came to commune in the Eucharistic sacrifice. This afternoon, Brother Luc receives two brothers for consultation. Father Gabriel Piroird talks of the figure of the Shepherd in the Bible. I read John again. When the hired man sees the wolf coming, he leaves his sheep and flees, and the wolf carries them off or scatters them, because a hired man doesn't worry much about the sheep. "I am the good shepherd, and I lay down my soul for the sheep. I have other sheep that do not belong to this fold."

[12/08/1994] Thursday, December 8th.

The holiest of dwellings. Love abides there. She is unshakable.

63. *Cf.* Tob 11:11-15.

and I, a sinner, go to her
Close to her I am
led into eternal life
conformed to truth
at peace, I go
surrendered to grace by the illumined gift I free
uttered in the recesses of your glorified body born of
the Most High
like Him
Christophe of Mary [in Arabic letters in the text]
I very close to your *I love you*
a disciple entrusted to the Gift
a brother given over to the Breath

forewarned acknowledged
invented inspired I baptized
simply said in the Gospel
here is your son
I re-born from on high here is your mother
communing connected enchanted
yes most beloved consecrated I Marie-Christophe go
to the Father
in Tibhirine
in the soil of Algeria
tender and violent
Abba close to Her here I am
[in Arabic in the text: *anâ huwa*]

[12/09/1994] Friday.

The end of the retreat was marked by the announcement of the death of Frédéric, 31 years old, Father Piroird's nephew.

[12/10/1994] Saturday.

If only I could keep in my heart two things I received during the retreat:

1. The loving, joyful, peace-giving closeness of Mary—near Her, Abba, here I am.

2. Trust cannot be "verified"; if you try to it vanishes. It ought to grow without ceasing and so becomes deeper. (Father Piroird)

[12/11/1994] Sunday.

Gaudete. Rejoice! Saint Christopher gets the honors in *La Croix-L'Événement*: front page, in full color, carrying Christ.

[12/13/1994] The 13th.

In chapter last night: how to formulate the votes of orientation before our bishop arrives? Some unrest around the "idea" that one single person—W. means me—might break ranks from the group in order to stay in Algeria as a response to the bishop's appeal. This morning I re-read Philippians: "May your love for each other increase more and more and never stop improving your knowledge and deepening your perception so that you can always recognize what is best."

It is not a question of putting together projects for establishing ourselves permanently here or there—nor, above all, of "imprisoning" the future, of controlling what is to come, something that Hope makes us believe is good, favorable. These votes are rather meant to clarify where we stand today by disposing us to receive what may come, not helter-skelter but based on our common convictions. The community becomes fully itself first of all in this experience of a common goal. I felt something like a temptation to turn in on ourselves to guarantee a safer outcome: finding ourselves all together in the end. It seems to me that would be a lack of greater love and, thus, of lucidness. A community is not called to secure survival for itself at all costs, but rather to give birth, to give life through the grace of the Spirit. "Woman, here is your Son. . . ." It's unexpected: the Gift enters the Church at that very hour of Calvary.

It seems to me we cannot exclude possible separations among us if there is a compulsory departure. Perhaps we ought to discuss that.

Compulsory separations if one or/and another . . . is murdered.

Underscore also what is at stake in this vote in case of the prior's physical death.

[12/14/1994] 12/14.

It's been one year since the death of the Croats at Tamesguida.

[12/15/1994] Thursday 15th.

Our bishop is expected for a time of discernment with us as Church.

". . . so that we despaired of coming through alive. Indeed, we had accepted within ourselves the sentence of death, that we might trust not in ourselves but in God who raises the dead. . . . In Him we have put our Hope" (2 Cor 1, 9-10).

[12/20/1994] Tuesday 20th.

Together with our bishop we have literally *been Church* in true mutual understanding. Gilles, Robert and Fernand opened the session—with the associates present as well. The gospel of the day is heard in Nazareth with Mary [Lk 1:26-38, the annunciation]. The impossible happens when trust gives it wide berth.

[12/24/1994] 12/24.

Elizabeth's "No!" before the whole clan impresses me: "No, he shall be called John." In order to truly come, Jesus' "Yes!" (to his Father) needs various freedoms that are determined, firm, unshakable, without being obstinate, because at bottom what is involved is obedience in the Breath.

[12/25/1994] Christmas today.

In Algiers, more than two hundred persons are taken hostage in an Airbus. For me, this Christmas is the Christmas of open arms. Last night, Christian in his homily contemplated the abandoned Child. At the Day Mass, Gilles emphasized the contrast between the words that formerly were said to the fathers (which seem to go backwards, to a figure of God, as an old man with a white beard) and the Child born of the Father, whose existence has never ceased to be turned toward Him.

[12/27/1994] The 27th.

Saint John, the disciple you loved, the table-companion closest to his threatened Rabbi.

[12/28/1994] The 28th.

Yesterday morning Fathers Chevillard, Dieulangard, C. Deckers and Christian Chessel were killed at Tizi Ouzou, offered up with the Friend they followed to the end.

"A Christian martyr is no accident. The martyrdom of a Christian is even less the result of a man's will to become a martyr, the way a man by strength of will and effort can become a leader.

"A martyr, a saint, is always created by God's design, through his love for humankind, to warn and guide them, to lead them onto his ways.

"A martyr is never the result of man's design, for the true martyr is one who has become God's instrument, who has lost his will in God's will, who has not lost it but found it, because he has found freedom in submitting to God.

"The martyr no longer desires anything for himself, not even the glory of undergoing martyrdom." (Thomas Becket)

Were they truly submitted to You, those four suicide-commandos at the Algiers airport? Truly Muslim[64] martyrs? Rachel weeps because *they are no more*. Our Church weeps, but her sorrow turns to joy: Paule-Hélène, Henri, Esther, Caridad, Alain, Jean, Charlie, Christian. They are ALIVE in your I AM.

64. "Muslim" is an Arabic word meaning "one who submits to God."

A stronger power entered the world after the angel's message to Mary: the power of being BORN that comes from God, which makes up the whole of his love story: you are my SON. Abba.

Make your kingdom come, Father: the SPIRIT, exactly where you want us.

[12/29/1994] The 29th.

At Vigils, I sang and I recognized your Song, your strength on my lips (will my heart ever fully be in tune, with precision and beauty?):

> *Gird your sword upon your hip, mighty warrior!*
> *In splendor and majesty ride on triumphant!*
> *In the cause of truth, meekness, and justice.*[65]

A. Charouqui translates this as: "Go and triumph, ride forth for the word of truth, humility and justice. . . . You love peace, you hate crime."

As a continuation of Gilles's homily on the word(s) of old to our fathers and Jesus-Word-newborn Child, from the same Psalm 44: "Sons shall be born to you in place of your fathers, princes . . ." (v. 17).

Christian will meet the Wali this morning.

[12/30/1994] Friday. Feast of the Holy Family.

Last night: Brother Luc and I were face to face, elevated together by a very tender power. I'm happy I had this dream. And I'm also happy for yesterday morning's work with Moussa, whose observations are astonishingly simple and upright. For example: "Nowadays there are some who read a couple of pages of the Koran and say: 'I am a Muslim'. Nevertheless the Koran says: 'One who kills the soul of his brother, lives in hell.' But in

65. Ps 44:4-5, NAB.

our time there is no future in sight, things are blocked. And if we could at least say of the four who were killed: these are the last ones. . . . Ah, if dying could stop and prevent the death of so many others, then I would gladly say: 'Yes, I volunteer.'"

[12/31/1994] 12/31/94.

A while back I made my simple vows for one year here. If I am (still) here today, it is thanks to You, it's grace upon grace. I remember, and the memory overflows. At Tizi Ouzou at 12 o'clock, a ceremony at the cemetery for our four brothers whom God loved so dearly that he gave them to Algeria as a sign of his great love for this country (Christian on Thursday), still so unsure of being really loved—which partly explains the violence that is shaking her. Our enclosure is definitely well protected: last night, a company of soldiers was imposed on us in order to guard us until late morning. What next?

1995

[01/01/1995]

Give us an attitude according to your heart: in truth.

Abba, next to Her, here I am.

Ordained a priest at Tibhirine, what have I made of this grace?

I begin this year . . . empty, on the edge of the absurd, whose motionless and confused extent I should recognize in myself. I must take my departure from the same place as you: descended into hell and risen on the third day.

There is time yet: I must LIVE you until all is accomplished. On with it! The Hour for this starts today.

At 10 o'clock today, at Our Lady of Africa, our wounded Church prays and celebrates the Eucharist in memory of You and your murdered disciples: Alain, Jean, Charlie, Christian.

[01/04/1995] The 4th.

Something has happened between Christian and me, as if his death has made us decide to be friends. Before that, I had only seen you twice, at the diocesan house in the priests' meetings. You were the youngest priest. We exchanged only a few words, but I am sure I met your gaze. Our eyes connected. What remains to me is the Light of this exchange, barely sketched but true.

Yesterday was the funeral with your family in France. The earth of Algeria is not jealous of this but rather the fuller for it. A friend, a Poor Clare from Algiers, has also left the country. Staying becomes something stronger, a grace of friendship: with

Him, this day. Trying to see ahead is illusory. The army surrounds us with its muscular arm. There are other arms in the mountain. To stay with the little people: this day.

You were slain, they told me, at mid-run, just about to go through the threshold. Now it is done. Existence is not a prison. The killers did not break your vitality.

Will you tell me whether it was their explicit intention—contaminated by a murderous madness—to take all of you hostage? I'd like to know. I'm wondering about the rest of this story in Algiers? in Tibhirine? A hostage takes the place of others, but it must be a free commitment so that this place (as victim) be filled with love, with FORGIVENESS. Only Jesus can draw us there, giving us a share in this place of the Son who is infinitely Brother.

Christian, five years ago (four years!) I was ordained a priest. I count on your friendship to help me to do well all that this ministry demands ("Do whatever he tells you," Jn 2:5), simply to become a priest living in obedience.

As your friend I must pray for your assassins.

Lauds. "My mouth laughs at my enemies." To ask this grace of the Word that is unarmed, naked, upright. "Whom are you looking for? *I am.*" Toward my Father. Yes, to cope by turning my face toward him as a son.

[01/07/1995] Saturday.

In Algiers, the day before yesterday, Sister Marie Bernard made the last act of her presence in this country, choosing to draw her last breath alone during the night. Her Poor Clare sisters are about to leave the monastery to go to Nîmes, where another place is awaiting them. "It's sad," Jean-Pierre said after the Eucharist, "everybody's leaving." Thursday, Célestin and W. are leaving for Morocco. Gospel of the wedding feast in Cana. It's like witnessing a marriage that's gravely compromised because hope is so absent. "Filling, pouring, taking," this is the task of servants, it's the work of friends: in (Marian) collusion as Church. Until a contrary sign is given, we're staying on as "wedding guests." I now copy these words from a letter from M.D.: "Their blood, their daily gift of themselves, seals this bond of peace rooted in the Life of God given in abundance on the Cross. Henri, Christian and so many others who remain unknown will be the root-work of the bond of Peace in God's eternity. May they help us to go on day by day in Hope, sometimes with that fear that is the lot of so many of our friends, sometimes with the feeling of futility, of the complete uselessness of what we're doing! Yes, we have to sink down deep into the faith, find again the roots of life in our own depths, the life we cannot give except by virtue of God's compassion for his suffering people" (Oran, December 28).

[01/08/1995] January 8th.

Your Epiphany—the manifestation of who you are.

[01/11/1995] Wednesday.

The world is a war zone. It isn't ideas, principles, abstractions confronting one other: it's Good against Evil, Life against Death, etc. There are two forces present, two antagonistic energies: two powers in competition. The power of Death is the decision to kill. The power of the Father is the decision to live. Love that begets the Son. On the Cross, the Son triumphs definitively. The Letter to the Hebrews says that by his death he reduces to impotence him who wielded the power of death. Standing firmly there, the Church is invested with the LIFE of the Son: "Woman, behold your Son." And the dragon resents the Woman who is giving birth.

[01/12/1995] Thursday.

The departure of Célestin and W., who were taken to the airport by Christian, leaves us more vulnerable. Something has come over the community: felt by each one in his own way.

[01/15/1995] Sunday.

Joy at Christian's return yesterday. At the Eucharist I preached on the Gospel of the wedding at Cana. "Life is a shipwreck," sang the hymn. Didier added a strophe: "Life is a marriage. . . ." On the phone (in Christian's office) a delightful surprise: Masako.

Hope is looking at things patiently, wishing others well and seeing things lucidly. Seeing the greatest things and heaven itself opening within pure hearts: the joy of the simple.

[01/16/1994] Monday.

Tonight the monastery is revealed to me as a school of peace. There is so much to learn from you. I think about a conversation with "my" dentist. "It's important that you exist." I object a little: but we're practically nothing at all and can be swept away. He says to me: "I'm thinking of you, but also of the imams, of religious men, whether they are Christians or Muslims." I sensed we represent something like a bulwark for him, something strong against Evil, resisting the chaos that seems about to engulf everything, beginning with meaning itself. Why shirk this expectation? The exigency persists: to become monk(s) here, in your crucified truth.

[01/17/1995] Tuesday.

Sant'Egidio[1] is getting involved in politics. That is their right. Jesus himself did not refuse to dialogue with either Judas or Pilate or the soldiers. Nevertheless, in him there is no ambiguity, no complicity: he bears witness to the crucified truth, he opposes murder—the homicidal lie—with the full force of a committed life: his body speaks by giving itself over, to affirm to the very end that unique power which he defends as he is being judged by man: Love as pure GIFT.

How could Sant'Egidio from now on claim to represent the legacy of Saint Francis and organize inter-religious encounters?

1. Named after the Church of Sant'Egidio (Saint Giles) in Rome, the Community of Sant'Egidio is a Catholic lay association, founded in 1968, with about 50,000 members worldwide. Its members are devoted to prayer, spreading the Gospel, service to the poor, and ecumenism.

In today's gospel, Jesus leads us through fields and frees in us the original gesture from before the Fall: gathering fruit. It's the gesture Cain could not stand in his brother. I haven't jotted down here what I overheard Mohammed, the caretaker, say one morning when it was snowing: "You see. His heart is all white. He sends us snow to make our hearts white."

I must listen more to what there is in the Islam of our neighbors that resists Evil.

Ramadan is coming up and is much awaited despite all its difficulties (like fasting in winter). It's the source of a misused hope. Is it the hope of seeing themselves again as Muslims without violent recriminations?

[01/19/1995] Thursday.

You order your disciples to keep a boat ready, in reserve, just in case. In the same way, our Church extends her care for us to the point of allotting us a second vehicle, to keep ready in reserve. But is this the best means of locomotion when the hour comes to pass over to the Other Shore, and in a hurry? I prefer your open arms: the Cross as emergency exit!

Yesterday, I happen to be there when the phone rings and I find myself on the line with Tamié: it's Jean-Marc, always kind and gracious, who tactfully passes the phone to Philippe [of Tamié], who's feeling a little down and troubled. He's a good friend, and was counting on coming here to escape an environment there that he resents as too security-minded, no risks ever taken! He tells me he'll live there as if he were here with us. Is this a good thing?

[01/22/1995] Sunday the 22nd.

Got back from Algiers yesterday, where I took part in a meeting with the priests of the diocese on Friday. A total immersion in the Church. The Cardinal said: "I am very tired, and now I will bless you together with the Archbishop." Yes, we were really blessed there, all together, in the Name of the Father and of the Son and of the Holy Spirit. The hierarchy is far from useless.

A minute ago A., the sheet-iron maker, asked for me. For nothing in particular. For the most essential thing of all: to see each other, to discuss the upheaval that's overwhelming and destroying us. "We pray for you, that God may protect us all. God be praised."

At the diocesan house, we affirmed these two convictions: 1. to refuse all violence; 2. to refuse all language implying exclusion. I certainly agree. But did we take sufficient stock of what saying this really involves? It means becoming a body without any complicity in murderous violence, witnessing to the (crucified) truth. And what kind of language are we to use when confronted with murderous words rejecting the stranger, the Communist, the Frenchman, the Christian crusader? Could poetry possibly have its own word—of peace—to sing on this battlefield?

[01/28/1995] Saturday 28th.

In the gospel: from one shore to the other, the adventure of our paschal faith. That one boat and the other boats. The Master asleep: you do not leave this world. You descend into hell: your faith reaches even there. So that everything will be gone through: you deliver us from fear. You are there in the trials of this world convulsed by so many squalls: humanity embarked on a stormy sea.

To stay on in Algeria, as close as possible to you: during this long Holy Saturday: "As the Father has loved me, I also have loved you: abide in my love."

Yesterday, a military operation in the neighborhood. And even more people killed. A. arrested yesterday.

[01/29/1995] Sunday.

Jesus, prophet of our today: give me the ear and the heart of a (beloved) disciple.

[01/30/1995] Monday.

Neighbors arrested (A. and M., A.'s two sons). A. released, but abandons his farm. In Algiers, a booby-trapped vehicle: 20 dead. A crucified people.

[01/31/1995] Tuesday.

Before Lauds I listen to Radio Algiers, Channel III. Provisional count: 38 dead. President Zéroual[2] wonders: "In the name of what ideology, in the name of what faith was this crime committed? In no other nation have I ever seen such barbarism. . . ."

[02/01/1995] February.

Beginning of Ramadan. Lord, give them a strong and generous "conviction of faith" (from the Letter to the Romans last night, while our neighbors entrusted this Ramadan to God, expressing to him a *riyya*, a "vision" intended to be unique and extending from this time until the last day).

[02/02/1995] 2/02.

An offering is present within the hollow expectations of the poor. To see you here where the pure Breath has brought me: for a decisive encounter, an outcome of peace: Now unbind your servant, according to the Gospel, in the PEACE of a surrendered love.

[02/05/1995] Sunday the 5th.

Yesterday, the 40th day of commemoration for Alain, Jean, Charlie and Christian (they died at Tizi Ouzou). A.'s son is still "detained." The gospel gives me 4 words, 4 verbs that commit me to you: to go out (into the deep), to cast forth (my life), to leave (everything) and to FOLLOW YOU. Follow you in your prayer: no one has gone further than you. "I go to the Father." "I give my life."

[02/06/1995] Monday.

So here we are on the shores of Islam. We're busy at our work and we can hear your call: "Go out into the deep," toward the

2. Liamine Zéroual, president of Algeria, 1994–1999.

great depths of an unknown and unpredictable Islam, beyond fundamentalist entrenchment and our own refusals and reductive prejudices.

Am I being called, I who know nothing in the field of Islamology? Little by little I find evidence of a great depth there. Maybe Muslims need the vision of a Christ-like friend to have that depth revealed to themselves and so be delivered from an inhuman and mendacious Islamism which seems to deceive the simple people so easily (?). As in the case of the attack in the Rue Didouche-Murad: it's written off as simply "bad luck" for the civilian victims since the target aimed at—the police—justifies the "means" (a 16-year-old boy was driving the car packed with explosives).

[02/08/1995] Wednesday.

Yesterday we started pruning the vines. Today, I am on retreat close by you, the true vine. In order to dwell in you as you dwell in me, and to produce the fruit that the Father expects of me. This morning I tasted the great joy—so very undeserved!—of being your beloved disciple. Near Mary most blessed I retrieve the great calm of my paschal origin: a plunge into the Love of the Trinity and the exigency of the Gift. The only thing necessary for the branch that has been pruned by the Word is to obey the divine sap completely. Explosions at about one o'clock this afternoon while I was reading Father A.-M. Carré's *Vient le temps de chanter* ["The Time for Singing Is Coming"].

In the middle of the afternoon, a piercing cry of distress, of humiliation (of humility) from our muezzin. From Father Carré: "In the hour of distress, one needs a trust that will dispel doubts." The trust of a child who dares to say 'Father!' "Faith is a life that wants to shape our acts to resemble Christ's."

"Will we never finish suffering? But the cross is also contemplation. Simply by not refusing we glimpse the face of God even now" (see *Marthe Robin*, by J.-J. Antier).

Armand Marquiset[3] writes: "With my soul that God has given me in order to love, I know that the greater the misery, the greater the desperation, the more you have to burn with love, the more you have to be ablaze with love—because if you are ablaze with love, you cannot avoid being ablaze with hope."

"Prayer," writes Bernanos, "is the only revolt that stays on its feet."

Cardinal Lustiger[4] once said to his candidates for ordination: "At this moment you are born again as priests. And this, your birthday to the priestly identity of Jesus for the sake of his priestly people, is a beginning which contains everything and where nothing is known, where everything is given and yet everything is still to be received."

"Whoever lets himself be worked over by the Word, dies young, no matter at what age." (Jean S.)

The Cross is the signature of the humble.

"To give what we have." (Claudel)

The "novelty" brought by Jesus: "I come to tell you what I have seen in my Father's house." P. 184: a time to listen to the song of the other.

[02/11/1995] The 11th. Saturday.

Our Lady of Lourdes and the gospel where your insides tremble at the sight of this crowd that has nothing. Lord, there are seven of us here. Take us and speak your thanksgiving over us who are next to nothing, and distribute it among those all around us.

Yesterday afternoon, a beautiful moment of exchange with M. and B.: the situation was very present, but re-situated within Your perspective, where each one receives the mission to give forth your Light, your Peace, your Love.

3. Armand Marquiset (1900–1981), French nobleman and philanthropist who founded a number of charitable organizations such as the Little Brothers of the Poor and the Friends of the Elderly.

4. Aaron Jean-Marie Lustiger (1926–2007), French convert from Judaism who became archbishop of Paris and a cardinal.

[02/12/1995] Sunday.

I'm not sure I got out on the right side of the bed this morning. Being with you does not at all depend on me and my (bad) moods. You have all the rest of today to persuade me to follow the happiness you suggest: "Blessed are you, the poor."

Happy like a tree is the friend who is planted near you
Let the season of the Fruit arrive. Come yourself! Cut, prune . . .

[02/13/1995] Monday 13th.

Yesterday, in his homily, like an echo of the words in the Magnificat, Christian spoke of God's happiness that turns everything upside-down.

On the phone: Mom, Dad and Claire.

[02/14/1995] Tuesday.

An overwhelming amount of mail: a correspondence oriented toward Joy.

[02/15/1995] Wednesday.

And the killing goes on. "To death with him, to death with him, crucify him."

[02/17/1995] Friday.

Geneviève B. tells me that Brother Placide has died—in his 96th year. I reread his letter, which I received three days ago in response to a message sent after the death of his catechism pupil, Sister Marie-Bernard of the Poor Clares of Algiers (Nîmes): "I don't forget you in my prayers. We have happy memories of your visit. United in prayer, with fraternal greetings and a friendly hug"—signed: "Br. M. Placide." Death in a monastery is a decisive moment that is lived in a simple way.

I liked the article by Father Gibert in *Christus*, no. 65: "Jesus in History and Faith." On page 63 I read: "One may justly marvel at the apophatic language of mystical theology, at the transcendental formulas common to various religions about what cannot be said of the divine, at the dazzling sayings that have been left to us by mystics of all the great religions; but nothing replaces God's plunge into human history, because he meets us exactly in what makes us most happily and tragically human, namely history. Because in the end the only point really is salvation, a salvation which humanity clamors for with all its might and at times with all its despair; a humanity that experiences itself throughout history as vulnerable, fragile and hurting, despite the joys that it may also taste."

Last night, I made a slip while talking to Moussa, when I said: "Your son didn't come," and I added: "You'll see, it will happen!" From the shower he replied: "I'm afraid not! *I really don't think so.*" For him it's impossible, and he has to learn to live with it. And he remains smiling and helpful: alive.

[02/22/1995] Wednesday.

Saint Peter's Chair. At Vigils I read what John Paul II says of his prayer as Pope. I love to see him like that. Last evening, we listened to Jean Vanier[5] concerning the vulnerability of Jesus, of the heart of God. He was pondering Jesus' heart-rending question: "And you, don't you want to go away?" (Jn 6). Such probing by the Gospel deeply touches me. Without judging the departure of any of the others, for myself to go away from this place would mean to stop walking with you, in your steps, committed as they are to this land of Algeria. I also hear this question as coming from my neighbors, from Moussa, from Mohammed and from Ali: Do you want to go away, to leave us? But the question comes from You and keeps me free in the Gift of the Father, binding me to you here. Will we have to leave one day?

Until then, never let me be separated from you. "Lord, to whom would we go?" You speak of living for ever.

5. Jean Vanier (b. 1928) is a Canadian Catholic philosopher, theologian, and humanitarian. He founded L'Arche, an international federation of communities for people with developmental disabilities and those who assist them.

Yes, Julien, you are within the truth of the Gospel—truly crucified—when you write to me: "You are doing your duty, and now no one can stop you any more, not even suffering, not even death." And you added: "Granpa and Granma think of you often, and are really very worried. But why all this worry, since the Lord is going to save us all. Give all the monks a hug from me."

[02/23/1995] 02/23.

On 01/22 Madame de Chergé wrote me: "I see all of you almost like the Child in the crib. You arrived at Tibhirine full of love. Look at you now, stripped of everything, completely deprived of action, isolated although surrounded by people, living with instability, risk, danger and poverty within the richness of Love. You are anticipating the day when with open arms, united with the cruciform arms of those who have fallen, you can all embrace in that peace that we love so much. [. . .] May the peace of the Lord put his joy deeply within each one of you, a serenity that instills peace in the face of gnawing fear and shattering separations."

There are rumors that about one hundred prisoners have been killed after a revolt that is said to have caused the death of four guards in a prison in Algiers.

[02/25/1995] Saturday.

"The GAZE of the Lord is upon those who love him; a powerful protection, a mighty support, a shelter from the desert wind, a shade from the midday blaze, a guard against obstacles, a safety against falling. He buoys up the spirits, gives light to the eyes, bestows health and life and blessing" (Sir 34:16-17).

Mohammed, Ali's son, said yesterday: "Ramadan is good. Some people tell me it's nothing but a hunger strike. No: you have to *feel* it, feel the hunger, feel the thirst."

"Christophe! Lent is coming soon. . . ."

[03/01/1995] Lent 1995. Ash Wednesday.

Last night in chapter, a real dialogue about violence and non-violence. Father Amédée and Christian talked about violence in children. One brother asked to be forgiven. Another one remembered Jean Vanier's thoughts on the hidden wound behind violence. We also discussed the need for patience with annoying and perplexing behaviors. Ever since his meeting with Salah Attia, Christian prays: "Disarm them!" And little by little this exigency has penetrated us as well: Disarm me, disarm us.

For my part, I see that the areas where my violence manifests itself to the prejudice of someone or other, and of the whole community, are also the areas where my violence might little by little experience conversion: in the liturgy, where song and word want to be prayer; in work, where much energy is given and spent; in community life, by the exercise of charity. I discover too that Hope is given us in our situation as an experience of radical non-violence with regard to time: by accepting that time escapes our control and our vain projects, we can open ourselves to the seeming Impossibility of a greater Love. Yes, anything could happen to us: coming from You and giving ourselves like you, in purity. An impossible resolution begins to take shape in my heart: "to love chastity," and to it I add this other instrument of good works: "to pray for one's enemies out of love for Christ." What lights the way is the dictum: "Happy are the pure of heart, for they shall see God." Up and at it, then! It's the hour of your Grace. May it be enough for me, I beg you, and draw me into your Passover.

Father, carry my soul in its carefreeness
To where you want, and let it sleep in your hand
Without asking the meaning and the goal of the road.

Free of all plans and know-how, let it be
Light, detached, and joyful upon awakening,
Like the gnats that dance in the sun.

Keep far from her a restless defiance
That measures the thread of the future ahead
Of you, and that weighs hope by past memories.

I surrender to You, divine Wisdom.
My strength will be at hand at the hour of need
Like the coat of a child well cared for by its mother.[6]

Marie Noël[7] *(The Hours. Prime).*

[03/02/1995] Thursday.

The face of Moussa this morning: happiness seeking to share, to communicate itself. It's *'Eid al-Fitr*.[8] And I am moved. He says: "*Hamdullah* ['Praise be to God!'] that God gave us a day together yesterday." But Ali, for his part, is annoyed: first, because he was unable to go and pray in a mosque because of the situation; and second, because he had seen on television that the president and his ministers were surrounded by body guards . . . for prayer.

[03/03/1995] Friday.

For the last two days I have been reading Tauler,[9] and am beginning this Lent in the sign of Christmas: being born, giving birth to the Word. Christmas is truly our grace as a community. We have to embrace it and allow it to bear fruit.

6. In the original French, the poem rhymes: "Père, porte mon âme en son insouciance / Jusqu'où tu veux et qu'elle dorme dans ta main / Sans demander le sens et le but du chemin. // Qu'elle soit, n'ayant plus ni dessein ni science / Légère, détachée, et joyeuse au réveil / Comme les moucherons qui dansent au soleil. // Détourne d'elle une inquiète défiance / Qui mesure avant toi le fil de l'avenir / Et qui pèse l'espoir avec le souvenir ; // Je m'abandonne à Toi, divine Sapience. / Ma force sera prête à l'heure du besoin / Comme un manteau d'enfant dont la mère a pris soin."

7. Marie Noël (1883–1967), pseudonym of Marie Rouget, French Catholic poet and mystic. Her work gives expression to a vivid struggle between deep faith and the temptation to despair.

8. "Festival of breaking of the fast," also called the Sugar Feast and the Lesser *'Eid*. An important religious holiday celebrated by Muslims worldwide. It marks the end of Ramadan, the Islamic holy month of fasting.

9. John Tauler (1300–1361), German Dominican, mystic, and theologian.

[03/05/1995] Sunday.

The Gospel in the desert: our better part, with you.

[03/06/1995] Monday.

If the Gospel really takes place in the desert—in the deserts of our earth and even in all its hells—it is because you, Jesus, have gone there docile to the Spirit: with full freedom. In order to oppose your freedom as Son to the grip of Evil. You were doing it there already. And you would do it thoroughly on the Cross. I am delivered from Evil. I smile before my impossible resolution to chastity. It is up to you to realize it in my weakness, which I wish to be humble, submissive, courageous. To love chastity. To want this freedom for your Love in me, for your salvation working through me here. To pray for your enemies (for love of you) is something that partakes of the chastity of a heart that is purified by the desire for the salvation of all, a heart that is detached, ungrasping: surrendered.

[03/07/1995] Tuesday.

Feast day: Perpetua and Felicity, holy martyrs. During Vigils we read the account of their martyrdom, a *true* liturgy. Will our own liturgy be led all the way to this Christ-like truth, completely saturated by his joy, his peace, the love that he gives us (rite of the kiss of peace)? A paschal liturgy: both the martyrs remain standing. The Office of the Cross. Perpetua, for her part, was to experience a particular pain:

being struck between the ribs
she let out a great cry.

. . . To live through such a way of being put to death
. . . she must have wanted it.

I cannot give myself a name other than my true name
I am a Christian Christophe
Here I am [in Arabic in the text: *anâ huwa*].

[03/09/1995] Thursday 03/09.

A firm resolution of abandonment—have I made it?—at bottom must come from your hands: into your hands I entrust myself completely.

The proper work of Hope is to open up time—despite all muddles, nights and fog—so as to keep it receptive to the Eternal. Father, may that happen to me.

[03/11/1995] Saturday.

Today you say to me in the gospel: Love your enemies. "Pray for those who persecute you. In order to be sons of your Father in heaven." Here, my double Lenten resolution receives from you all its weight both of bliss and of impossible demands. What's at stake is love: non-exclusive, unlimited. Excessive love. Prayer for those who kill people (they haven't threatened us explicitly yet, despite the arms they undoubtedly were ready to use against us) sustains our relationship with them. It also disposes us interiorly and identifies us as sons of the Father with regard to brothers who are also his beloved sons. It's a Marian prayer, consisting of both resistance and submission. Chastity becomes a weapon of non-violence in the context of enemies and persecutions; it becomes an opening of the heart stronger than the withdrawal into oneself proper to the egotistical and narcissistic affect.

[03/12/1995] Sunday.

A prophetic dream last night! During a concelebration in a cathedral—a ceremony organized by the archpriest, Julien O.!—I turn to my neighbor who's in priestly vestments (chasuble): it's Sister Odette! These events are surely turning us into a priestly people. "What has changed in you?" Father Lépine asked Christian. This is the question that brings us together in chapter this morning, and I am happy we're having this community dialogue: "This one—here among us, giving Meaning to our presence here—is my beloved Son. Listen to him."

[03/13/1995] Monday.

On the mountain your face changes. The change comes from within, from where the Father is speaking to you, gazing on you. What becomes manifest to the eyes of the disciples is that at bottom you are ALL FACE, turned toward the Father and drawing us into your light. Pure hearts are hearts that are susceptible to that Light. They abide in the ultimate illumination: in the (resplendent) truth. In chapter yesterday morning, a very soft light shone among us: we were "all gaze" as we listened to one another, listening to you.

[03/14/1995] Tuesday.

Perhaps it's not enough to say that we don't have to choose between the powers that be and the terrorists. As a matter of fact, every day we already make the concrete choice in favor of those Jean-Pierre calls "the little people." We cannot stay if we cut ourselves off from them. That makes us depend, in part, on their choice concerning us. We could become troublesome to them tomorrow or later on. Jesus on the cross is rejected also by the people, but by no means by all. It's not numbers that count.

Today's gospel: only one Teacher, the Spirit who teaches us Jesus Christ, our only Master. Only He reveals to us the only Father.

[03/19/1995] Sunday.

We have started using the chapel again—restored and shiny-new inside. For three days the novitiate sheltered your Presence. This morning I become aware of the extent of my charge as father-master, and how much it is beyond me, inviting me to go into the beyond obedience makes possible. Does this fig tree bear any fruit? It's not for me to know; but I do believe more and more that the Master is waiting for the fruit that my life alone can offer him freely, for his Joy. Before the Eucharist, a meeting between Christian and me within the poverty of obedience. But from now until the elections of . . . March '96, so many things can happen and be a sign to us. We are also experiencing freedom as regards the future: the future of Algeria and of our community at Tibhirine-Fez, and of myself among the other brothers, each of whom has his own history. Christian is free to want to leave his position as prior to someone else. I for my part feel called to become simply "I" in YOUR crucified truth: *I love you.*

Saint Joseph. Happy the faithful servant! God entrusts his household to him: the Child and his Mother and the whole earth. Anniversary of my consecration to Mary, at Tamié (in 1975?). Joseph, to you I entrust our house here and in Fez, and also the care of my two (impossible) Lenten resolutions (chastity and prayer in Christ for enemies).

[03/26/1995] Sunday 26th.

Yes, I arise, I begin to be your son. And the most beautiful thing is what happens to me in your arms. I was very happy and moved during the Eucharist of the Annunciation, presided over by our Shepherd, who is here with us celebrating his 40 years of service. Surely, he has been led where his temperament would not have led him, and here he is, dispossessed, stripped of everything, hurting. He does not seem to be "possessed" by a "vision" of our future—the Church of Job. A Church at the mercy of a human family. A Spanish priest who was here for a few days remarked that, for once, we were able to talk about a new evangelization.

[04/06/1995] April 6th.

The meeting of the Ribât last week, the return of our brother Célestin, and today Christian's departure are so many happenings that call to me in special ways. Tonight I have the task of dispensing love to my brothers, to those who share our work and our life, to R., to Tihirine and to the Algerian people. Yesterday morning Christian told us how he responded in Algiers to the question: "What is your experience of God in the present situation?" He stated five convictions: God accompanies us, and so I am being led. God is silent, while others speak for him. God has a horror of death. God scorns no creature. God loves the Algerians, *versus* the results of a poll among the French. By sharing this, Christian is inviting us to go into Holy Week with this question.

In the afternoon I speak with M., and then with M., who have heard talk of the pirate television broadcast by the GIA of a "reportage" about their army. I realize how affected and vulnerable they are. The arguments seduce and deceive them, while I can't say anything. I dared to utter the word "propaganda"! Jesus: in you there is no complicity with the Lie and its decision to kill. But to the end you remain open like a guest at table. Oh, do not let me ever leave your table. Hold me very tight to your heart as a beloved disciple.

[04/09/1995] Palm and Passion Sunday.

In the mail I read a letter from Jean Corbon[10] (addressed to Christian), and then Mom talking about Dad who is very weak and is on oxygen, and then Georgette from Lebanon and M.-Ch. from the abbey of Désert. These letters draw me to where you are pure PRAYER, stripped of all liturgical "vestments" (antiphons, responses, hymns, etc.)! . . . with which I'm fed up, as you well know. Holding on until EASTER! Help me.

G.: "I surrender my heart to Scripture. Jesus Christ is at the heart of our pierced friendship."

I enjoy reading *Actualité religieuse* (no. 131). Guy Coq asks: "How do you love?" The thirst for loving. G.C. speaks of a film: *À travers les oliviers* ["Through the Olive Trees"].[11] I'm not going to see it. I think that I might recognize myself in it: there is Hossein, in love with a young girl who doesn't reciprocate, but at the same time leaves the way open to non-refusal.

10. Jean Corbon (1924–2001) was the principal author of the section on prayer in the *Catechism of the Catholic Church*. He was a Dominican of the Greek-Catholic eparchy of Beirut who tightly integrated Eastern and Western theology. He is best known for *The Wellspring of Worship* (Ignatius, 2005), a masterful treatise on the fundamentals of the eucharistic liturgy.

11. Iranian film directed by Abbas Kiarostami (1994).

My whole existence plunged into this plot wholeheartedly. I exist as an "offering of love." In a very stark way this tale portrays the very essence of the search for love. With a certain symbolic transparency, it points to an analogous quest—the quest for a God who seems to keep silent. It's always the same waiting, the same love in suspense. Sometimes we are on the verge of the response, but we must return toward the truth of prayer. There is also an interview with Raimon Panikkar:[12] "The Church as a place of salvation: wherever the divine mystery of salvation touches men, there is the Church. [. . .] The Mass celebrates, re-enacts something that belongs to the whole of humankind. To recognize that Christ—he whom I call Christ in my language and who for me is truly the Risen Jesus—comes to make all traditions fruitful. The price to pay for this choice is a new *kenosis*,[13] an annihilation of Christ." He contrasts inter-religious dialogue (concerning doctrine) with intra-religious dialogue. Finally, I do think that at least one word hit home and continues to nourish me from the really long sermon we heard after the Passion story, read by Paul with such moving and gentle sincerity. Yes, Jean-Pierre began with a meditation on the silent cry that is characteristic of Christian faith: "Blessed is he who comes in the name of the Lord." Awe-struck recognition of who You are. To put ourselves at others' disposal . . . here, in Algeria.

[04/10/1995] Monday.

Brother Luc is amazing. This morning, before Lauds, he treats those come, and then tells them not to come back "during Holy Week"—unless they are very tired. . . .

12. Raimon Panikkar (1918–2010), Indian-Catalan Catholic priest and writer, proponent of inter-religious dialogue.

13. In Christian theology, *kenosis* is the concept of the "self-emptying" of one's own will and becoming entirely receptive to God and his perfect will, following the example of Christ himself. It is used both as an explanation of the Incarnation and an indication of the nature of God's activity and condescension. See Philippians 2:5-7.

[04/13/1995] Holy Thursday.

[04/14/1995] Good Friday.

You offered yourself to the Father through the eternal Spirit.
Purify my conscience
of dead works by your blood
so that I can serve here
O LIVING GOD (*cf.* Heb 9:14).

[04/15/1995] Holy Saturday.

Happy EASTER, Jean-Pierre says to me after having GIVEN me absolution. Returning to one of my two Lenten resolutions—to love chastity—Jean-Pierre points out that purity of heart suffices because it draws all the rest in its wake (silence, obedience, poverty, charity . . .). Yesterday afternoon, I asked the Father, in the name of Jesus, for the grace of humility. Am I receptive to his Fire?

[04/23/1995] The 23rd.

It is EASTER: you are alive, and your PEACE—that comes to us from the Father and the Breath—inspires us to live here through, with and in you. The whole week also is the octave, which is somewhat exhausting . . . for everybody, but especially for the cantor. Yesterday, we got no. 91 of the journal *Liturgie.* I can hear W. there, speaking in Psalm 38.

P. 338: Jesus does not deliberately seek this situation of being excluded, but when it finally is imposed on him he does not refuse it. (He says in v. 13: "In your house I am a passing guest, a pilgrim.") Why? Because he already is aware to what extent the Father also is involved, in the heart of his Son, in this death that is foretold. Also, the moment when Jesus has penetrated to the depth of the misery of man in God, is for him exactly the moment when he returned to the bosom of the Father.

Ever since that day, in every situation where God has apparently withdrawn himself, there is present the face of the abandoned Christ, and in that face there is proof of God's incomprehensible closeness. Paradoxically, the more one distances oneself, the closer he is.

(For example, there in Algiers yesterday, when the killers murdered a woman who was professor of architecture at the polytechnical school, a colleague of Abderahman.)

> because we can't even begin to fathom how far Jesus went . . .
>
> There is no degradation or abandonment that he has not known, and that he has not transformed, by his presence, into a place of closeness to God.

I also enjoyed this quote from Guardini:[14] "The meaning we attribute to liturgical acts (by declaring that they signify this or that) may be profound, but it is only a creation of our mind, whereas that meaning ought to be deduced, in living fashion, from the acts themselves. For, in the liturgy, ideas do not hold first place but derive from the reality itself: not yesterday's reality but today's, a reality that is being renewed continually in us and through us; in short, a reality that is human in both its form and its behavior. Liturgy is a world that has taken shape, a world of sacred and hidden events. It is sacramental. It is above all a question of learning that living act through which the believer conceives, receives and enacts the sacred and visible signs of invisible Grace."

[05/02/1995] May 2nd.

I have left this journal aside to keep the community chronicle up to date in Christian's absence. He was on the phone yesterday morning and is supposed to be coming back Thursday, *hamdullah* ["Praise God!"]. The pastoral burden is a real burden. My shoulders and, even more so my heart, are not broad enough.

14. Romano Guardini (1885–1968), German Catholic priest and author.

[05/07/1995] Sunday 7th.

We live together in a land of hope. We cultivate it. We are dwellers in your house. We live there. We pray there. We abide there until it's time to die. We live together in your hand. Who could dislodge us from this blatant happiness? During Office this spontaneous prayer arises—is it from my heart? *On my lips: my God.* I'm fed up with the Office. It's a distaste in me that goes way beyond any judgment of my neighbor. Tomorrow is the 8th.

[05/08/1995] Monday, May 8th.

Brother Henri and Sister Paule-Hélène are free in the Gift that overtook them (took them over) in the Kasbah in the midst of their service. Today we hear Jn 10:1-10. "It is I who am the gate." Anyone who enters through me will be safe. He will go freely in and out, sure of finding pasture. To be your disciple means to be here, in Tibhirine—on this very morning: through you and out of you. I have come into Algeria through this gate. We have great freedom to go at our own speed, like you. You have come that all may have life, and have it completely. The point is being here like people who have their life from you, to the extreme of shedding all self-interest. To come to Algeria through you is a movement of infinite and precise love: Go, love this people, be the servant of my *I love you.*

[05/10/1995] The 10th.

'Eid al-Kebir.[15] "You have given me a body, so I say to you: Here I am, I am coming." I am coming to you, Father, in Jesus through the Breath that he gives me: his life as your Son.

15. One of the most important feasts *('eid)* in Islam. *'Eid al-Kebir* means "the Greater Festival" (by contrast to "the Lesser Feast," *'Eid al-Fitr,* the festival that breaks the fast at the end of Ramadan). Its proper name is *'Eid al-Adha* ("festival of the sacrifice"). It commemorates Abraham's faith and obedience as he prepares to sacrifice his firstborn son Ishmael as an act of submission to God's will.

On Sunday I said that Brother C. cannot be the center of our community. But he has the right—in Christ—to be its heart, because he is poor. I hope the meeting of us "cantors" just now may go well! After supper yesterday, a prophetic vision: in the yard, under the scriptorium window, Rabah and his little sister Kenza were watering two (dead?) branches that they had just planted: yes, on them your face fills with light. And this Light feeds my hope. The tree with birds will grow, in spite of everything. How broad the opening in me when I hear what you say—not from yourself, but as it is said transcendentally—at the source—in your Father: "He who believes in me, believes not in me, but . . ." I must accept seeing every "object" of faith fade out like this and slip away. One must go through this night of faith in order to be drawn all the way to Him who sends you, to whom you entrust yourself completely; and so you lead all human faith to its fulfillment in love. But the Father himself vanishes: "This is my beloved Son, listen to him."

[05/13/1995] In Fez, kingdom of Morocco.

Left Tibhirine on Thursday, after a first take-off . . . we landed again. Then I took the plane on Friday, and only arrived this morning at 12.15 a.m. in Fez, because there was a train strike. There is always a tacit agreement in the cloister to bring things up to date, if one of us has as much as set foot in the outside world; but it occurs as if by interior self-evidence. And I feel at home here with my brothers Jean-Baptiste, Jean de la Croix and Bruno. W. is at Meknes. During chapter I sensed there are certain questions about him: and after these "liberties," what's in his future? And what about relationships? I hope we can meet somehow in the truth of things. I must be watchful in fostering this desire.

On the bus between Casablanca and Fez, a good conversation with Mohammed, a Tunisian who studies computer science in Fez. He fell asleep, and after that we lost contact. I reproach myself for withdrawing so swiftly from the conversation. I didn't really say a proper good-bye to him.

[05/14/1995] Sunday.

Your LIFE among us: our fraternal life! Joy and Light. X. is on his way here: you accompany him. Sophie was baptized in Ancône. The phone is out of order, so we cannot get through to Tibhirine in Algeria. Such separation opens one's heart to a more unselfish communion. Marc's presence here is beautiful: it partakes of your beauty, that of the Servant who's been humiliated, raised up again and glorified. Yes, we monks come from afar, from far down. Without your hand, I plunge back into the abyss. Father Jean de la Croix generously gives me things to read! I've begun reading Julian of Norwich[16] in the edition of B. Sesboüé, *Pédagogie du Christ* (["Christ's Pedagogy"], Seuil).

[05/16/1995] Tuesday before Lauds.

X. arrived yesterday, an hour before Vigils. I must be present to him, with all my heart: both of us receptive to the Holy Spirit, brothers in Christ's own obedience, children of God, yes, our Abba every day.

The wound of Algeria pierces me. I am happy it is so.

[05/17/1995] The 17th.

By a strange coincidence, X. and I are both ill tonight. We can't go to Meknes to see W. X.'s frailty pervades his features like a translucent sadness. We say nothing important to one another. I can only offer him a glance that is fraternal, not haughty. I want to embrace what You want to give me during these days in Fez.

[05/20/1995] Saturday 20th.

Now I seem to have slipped nicely into the simple life that I am offered in this house of grace. I pray that I may be steeped in it. Jesus said: "I go away and I will return." To leave Algeria

16. Fourteenth-century English anchoress, mystic, and writer.

might well lead me more deeply into a closeness of love for this people that I have, in fact, already withdrawn from, leaving it to its history. Yes, I have distanced myself from this people for a while. Now I go to the sidelines in order to see to a task occurring within me and that has to do with X.'s journey, which nevertheless concerns Algeria. I am a monk of Tibhirine-Fez. That's how I spontaneously signed the first letter I wrote here.

The other morning, when I saw the sight—long forgotten!—of myself in a mirror over the washbasin in my room (what luxury!), I discovered a few definite wrinkles on my forehead, which must apparently belong to me.

Before Compline I talked with Christian, on the phone from Tibhirine: questions about the regular visitation and the "election." I hope this last question doesn't become too dominant. What concerns me more is Brother Célestin's health (insomnia, etc.), mysteriously reflecting Algeria's suffering. (The high-voltage electricity pylons have been cut down . . .)

As for X., there are certain signs that need interpreting, and since they concern his relationship with me, it's also me they call into question. And in this connection, too, there's a violence that must be faced without running away and without allowing myself to be overwhelmed by the violence lurking within myself. Mary, standing upright at the heart of the violence: she is full of hope.

[05/21/1995] Sunday.

This morning, an unclouded meeting with X. Tonight I read these words in a letter from Ágnes to Mónika (Letter 60, *Correspondence 1961-62.* Mónika Tímár,[17] in: *Vie consacrée*, 11, 1995). "Few people really know how to love. You must know how to be pa-

17. Mónika Tímár (d. 1962) was a Hungarian Cistercian nun and member of an underground community in the 1950s, after the Communist government prohibited all religious orders. Her journal was smuggled out of Hungary and translated into French, Italian, and German. Hans Urs von Balthasar wrote an introduction for the German edition. See: http://www.cistercian.org/abbey/history/our-saintly-inspiration/monika-timar.html.

tient, to have a deep respect for the other's countenance, and to help only in making his own features become more patent."

Things went very well with M., too: a very human exchange. Lord, accompany him on his journey, so that he may taste the joy of giving his life instead of seeing it escape from him, leaving him alone, on the sidelines. I get the impression he is in his right place here: not as a "monk," but integrating in himself, in his own way, the values that characterize our existence: service, the interior life, prayer (but I am not a church mouse myself!), fraternal living. No doubt his experiences as a family brother at Arles, then at Aiguebelle, have given him the impression that he is not fully embraced but only being used. He is aware of his limitations.

[05/23/1995] Tuesday.

Julian of Norwich communicates to me her desire, received from You: to see MARY. And this spiritual gaze passes through you: to become conformed to you and to see her truly as my holy Mother: in the shadow of the Spirit, at the foot of the cross, and glorified in the joy of Love.

[05/24/1995] Wednesday.

Yes, Mary, you know my desire to see you—me, a sinner—in your beauty. "Take off your robe of mourning and misery; put on the beauty of God's glory forever. Don the cloak of God's justice, bear on your head the diadem of the glory of the Eternal. For God wants to show all the earth your splendor: you will be named by God forever 'the Peace of justice,' 'the Glory of devotion'" (Baruch 5).

At the end of supper, Guy tells us that a young woman, a journalist, has been murdered in front of her family, in Algeria.

I want to see you, Mary, in prayer, as an *orans*[18] full of grace, adoring in Spirit and truth.

18. Figure of a woman, praying with arms outstretched, in ancient Christian iconography.

The Breath of truth comes. Mary was the first to be overwhelmed by it. It communicates to us what must happen. All that happens to us is included in it, embraced in the Love-Happening-Gift.

[05/25/1995] Thursday.

We shall celebrate your Ascension on Sunday.

To see Mary in the splendor of your design, Abba: fully in accord with your Desire. Close to her, I receive from your son my place as disciple. Here I am. I come.

[05/26/1995] Friday.

I have begun reading *Un moine de l'Église d'Orient* ["A Monk of the Eastern Church"], by Élisabeth Behr-Sigel, Éditions du Cerf.[19] On p. 103 I read: "There are 'constructive' vocations that found, establish and develop, and then there are vocations of 'loss' that achieve no positive results and desire 'loss' (in the full sense of the word) in order to find themselves" (Letter to O. Rousseau).

[05/27/1995] Saturday 27th.

Right in our midst, here and at Tibhirine, something is happening, something is to be done, that has the Word made flesh as its origin and guarantor: it is you, the risen Jesus, my Lord.

It's not a question of jumping ahead, but of being prepared. Prepared for everything. Am I really prepared? Detached? Rid of all personal ambition? The work is accomplished on a cross. To prefer nothing to your work. Julian of Norwich writes: "He

19. English translation: *Lev Gillet: A Monk of the Eastern Church* (Oxford, 1999), a biography of Archimandrite Lev Gillet (1893–1980). Brought up as a Roman Catholic, he became a Benedictine monk in Clermont, Luxembourg, and signed his books "a monk of the Eastern Church." Later, in England, he joined the Russian Orthodox Church and was widely known as a spiritual writer and promoter of Christian unity.

does not want us to be crushed by the suffering of the storms that are hammering us. These always come before the miracles" (p. 127). The FATHER himself loves you, because you have loved me and have believed that I have come from God. Now I leave the world and go to the Father.

[05/28/1995] Your Ascension, Lord.

"Whoever turns his freedom over to the Lord, adores him, and receives the freedom of the children of God. He loves as the Lord loves, and will be carried off as a captive of the invisible divine freedom." (Thomas Merton)

In order to come to You and commune with your movement of filial freedom, I must first descend and become a disciple-no-greater than his rabbi. With you, we ascend through humility. Show me, Lord, the trajectory of the ladder that has been raised: the degrees of humility that you expect of me, your disciple. To aspire to descend has nothing about it of a (morbid) taste for nothingness or the negative; it means choosing the only way to go up. Little Thérèse would say it's choosing the divine Elevator. It's to see the vanity of all willful "ascents." It is a crucifying choice. A beautiful meeting with X., full of trust. I must be very careful and not take more space than he gives me. I might awaken his fears, his violence. To be humble in this relationship: to allow your love to do everything well. A good, long walk with Bruno. The beauty of Fez, and the human misery. Much conviviality in the streets.

[05/29/1995] Monday, desert day.

I got a biblical light on the "vision" I received at Tibhirine the night before I left: "It is I, Yahweh, who cut down the tree that is standing, and raise up the one that is cut down, who make the green tree dry up and the dry tree flower."

Yesterday Sophie was baptized: a happiness that I share. Separated from all, *united* to all. Julian writes: "He wants us to know that he is the foundation of our life of love, and even more, he is our custodian of eternity" (p. 133).

Jn 16:32-33: "But I am not alone, because the Father is with me. I have told you all this so that you might have peace in me." [The Son introduces his own into—and keeps them in—a new space of existence that is characterized by the divine gift of peace.] Am re-reading my notes on John Paul II's encyclical, *The Gospel of Life.* They awaken reflections that are most relevant to the Algerian reality: the place where we live our life. First, there is the fact that we are a community that is *alive,* and this is a paschal experience. Here, John Paul II is at one with us: to choose life is a fundamental orientation. Or when he underscores the lived contrast between the precariousness of life and the affirmation of its value. Yes, our existence affirms life in a context where killing is routine.

We are a community (Church) marked by the sign of the blood of the Lamb. After the murders of Henri and Paule-Hélène, our Christian community is marked, just like the people at large, by this shed blood—shed unjustly by the assassins and quite often courageously offered by their innocent victims. And then there is the blood of Christ, which gives life and offers us communion in eternal life.

The cup: where the gift is given to us to live in you, with you, through you. In each Eucharist we celebrate LIFE: the victory of the Living One over against those who kill. This *celebration* overflows into a *service of charity,* exercised by each one according to the measure of his gift of faith: "caring for all life, and for the life of all." Indeed, this is a task lived out at the dispensary, at the gate, in the kitchen, or in the garden.

This service is situated within fidelity to the love that is experienced in that way: one cannot simply forget and leave without betraying what remains a grace of closeness, of friendship, of truth.

A community that is alive—and that has resolutely decided for life. In spite of, and even by virtue of, the signs of our ageing, I sense that each one of us is truly alive, and using our freedom in order to live—until we die.

I rather feel that we are in the process of being born, and it seems to me that a special effort should be made to be vigilant, to be available, to be attentive: the most precious thing may yet happen to us at the very heart of the worst.

A community facing Evil: we experience that something within us puts up resistance: someone in our midst confronts the aggression, offering his face of peace and open hands.

John Paul II would be pleased with us, I think: Someone is being proclaimed. To be precise—thanks to my reading of the life of Father Lev Gillet—the subject of the proclamation, the subject of this spiritual life at Tibhirine, is the Holy Spirit. That delivers us from any kind of heroism, indeed from all aspiration to seeing our names in the martyrology.

A fighting community, yes: but unarmed and affirming a true space of lived fraternal peace, where the Prayer of the risen Jesus takes place, creating a locus of PEACE. This, in turn, demands from us a great concern for the truth: without smugness and without complicity with the murderous Lie.

A Marian community, close to the Cross, attentive to the life that is about to be (re)born.

"The only one who remained standing in the hour of affliction was the one who, the night before, had bent his head to rest it on your breast" (Father Lev Gillet, p. 311). I want to rest my head on you, here in Fez.

Sacramental encounter, in which I hear you say to me in truth (in our fraternal Church): I forgive you all your sins. Before that, in the Gospel, I opened the book to the place where you say to Zacchaeus: "Zacchaeus-Christophe, hurry, come down, because I must stay at your house today." May your Spirit, O Jesus, impress in me your eagerness to come down, and deliver me from pride, so that I may live at eye level with others as a simple brother, an artisan of Hope. O my God, you are our secure hope [in Arabic in the text: *Allah humma anta rajâ 'unâ*].

to be born (the hope that comes to me)
  with you   everything begins   finally
  yesterday is let go of   today is free
  in the opening   a future of light takes shape

your likeness   draws me
I have slipped   into your Pasch
and I allow myself   to be taken up completely into
    your life
your resurrection   invades me
    through you the gift becomes real
    and joy makes everything eternal
gospel and poem according to you
my length of days
becomes etched word by word   step by step
in the benevolent heart of a woman   standing   there
monk ordained priest   I emerge from the love
that transfixes her   near her   close to the body
crucified by a people you love   I am
grounded in hope by my vows
truly in the depth of my being—breath and prayer—it is
    you, the servant
who enchants me.   Onwards now—obeying is the sole
    adventure
        Abba I come   I arrive quickly.

[05/31/1995]

You, Lord, give me the grace of your praise.

Clinging close to Mary. Joy.

Yesterday, Saint Joan of Arc. In the afternoon I get a parcel: 2 pullovers, knitted by Mom. A gift on her feast day. An invitation to communicate through distances—with detachment—in crucified Love, in you, the Risen Lord. Last night's dream: does it foretell better days? Brother Robert threw a barbecue party. For what reason?

On May 29, 1930: Brother Jean-Baptiste's first vows.

Commenting on the passage in the Gospel (Lk 1:39-45), Father Lev Gillet concludes: "Thus, what is of God in every man and in every religion can recognize what is of God in another religion" (p. 516).

[06/02/1995] Friday.

Yesterday Thami and I went for a long walk in the surrounding towns (Medina, Fesjdid—a new town). I feel at home with this simple and upright man. He is on the side of the little ones, of the humble you raise up. Tonight, I read a letter of Christian's, who forwarded a letter from Camille. I am still shaken. Lord, what direction will things take? Today we hear Jn 21:15-19. "Do you love me?" "Feed my sheep," "Follow me" [in Arabic in the text: *'a tuhibbunî—îr'a himlanî—itba 'nî*].

A living community "engenders" by the Gift received, accepted, believed in, hoped and waited for. I also read the text written at Atlas for the newsletter of the Rîbat and signed "Brother Christophe"; but the self-effacement of the transcriber is like a spiritual engendering. Yes, in that very relationship, but it's useless to belabor the point. I give you thanks. Lead this relationship, which is already good and beautiful, to the full extent of truth, which is LOVE.

Last Thursday, during our Arabic "course," A.'s face suddenly became closed and hardened when talking about the professors at the university (except one): they are not professors; we have no relationship with them; they don't respect us; in fact, they despise us. Yes, behind the happy and smiling face of this people, there seems to be a background of suppressed anger, a thirst for justice.

Thami told me about his house yesterday. He's finished building the ground floor for the owner of the plot. He still has to build his own house (second floor), and that'll be, he said, "*dar el-malik*—'the palace of a king!'"

[06/03/1995] Saturday.

An evening at the Little Sisters' with X. Eucharist, meal, sharing of our lives. This is how X. comments on the gospel during this sharing: "This gospel leaves me empty." I'd like to ask *him* that question ("Do you love me?"). In the building, we hear Edith Piaf's voice somewhere: *Non, je ne regrette rien!*[20]

Today this question is on my mind: Lord, what will become of X.? May he receive the Gift: joy and peace in the Spirit.

I wonder what my share of influence is (deriving from either my role or the self I cannot change) in those depressive phrases of X. that so disturb me. . . .

[06/04/1995] Pentecost.

Abba, grant that I may live like one risen, between your two Hands—the beloved Son and the Holy Spirit. May I reach out toward life and peace, drawn by what is humble, obedient to the GIFT, in conformity with Christ my Savior.

May I never *sadden* your Breath of joy, nor *resist* its Power, nor *extinguish* its Flame of love in me or in any creature on whom it rests.

> O Love, I surrender to Thee with all my freedom, my spirit, my heart and my will. I want to be subject to Thee because where the Spirit of the Lord is, there is freedom. There is no other true freedom. I want to be set free from servitude to my own will, a false freedom which is the worst slavery of the soul. To be Thy servant is to possess the freedom of the children of God.
>
> O Holy Spirit of God, take me as Thy disciple, guide me, illuminate me, sanctify me, bind my hands that I may not do evil, cover my eyes that I may not see it; sanctify my heart that evil may not rest within me.
>
> Be Thou my God, be Thou my Guide; wheresoever Thou leadest me, I will go; whatsoever Thou forbiddest me, I will renounce; and whatsoever Thou commandest, in Thy strength I will do. (Cardinal Manning[21])

20. Edith Piaf (1915–1963), internationally famous French popular singer of *chansons* and ballads, often on the themes of love, loss, and sorrow, of which *Non, je ne regrette rien* ("No, I regret nothing," 1960) is one of the best known.

21. Henry Edward Manning (1808–1892), English Catholic archbishop of Westminster and cardinal.

Abba Jesus

all my life is drawn there, into the Fire of this open Relationship: may all have LIFE.

all my existence is a wager on the truth of this admirable exchange,

everything comes to me within this GIFT, this Happening,

everything takes its course in peace.

Beautiful Eucharist. X. is sufficiently relaxed to play the *kora*[22] and tell us about an impulse for prayer. We had a good exchange touching on the real questions. Will we be able to accept the invitation from the sisters at Taza? There are four of us here today. Bruno and Guy are at the closing of the Synod. I was able to talk to Élisabeth on the phone this morning, and to Christian in the afternoon. Now I'm beginning to think about my return (on the 26th).

Without rushing ahead in any fanciful way, I should let myself be drawn more deeply to these words: "As the Father has sent me, I also send you."

As regards X.: I should act according to this other will that grips me and detaches me beyond all illusory influence. I must share your call without imposing it.

[06/05/1995] Monday.

At Tibhirine, Célestin is quite ill. I bring his suffering into relationship with X.'s and Camille's vocation. A living community means also this transmission of life through the pangs of birth.

[06/06/1995] Tuesday.

Father, Abba, by the marvel of your grace I can SURRENDER TO YOU

yes, in Jesus, your Son: to give myself over to You completely.

22. The *kora* is a 21-string bridge-harp used extensively in North and West Africa.

It's a way of the cross, I see that: one must travel it, completely given over (to the Spirit)

as a child in your hands
yes, I go to You
I come.

[06/07/1995] The 7th.

Before Lauds I read a letter from a young Pole, Michal Ziolo, 34 years old (born in March, 1961) who feels called to live the Cistercian monastic life at Fez. Last night I received Brother Célestin's deeply moving words. *I am sure* his suffering is bearing fruit. Lord, cure him so that all that remains in him is *the greater love* toward which you are drawing us.

To listen to the Spirit: to what he says to us, the community of Fez-Tibhirine. To come up with a way of responding. Yes, I have the sense of being a brother in a community whose life is from You. So, we've got to give ourselves over to this work: to be born, to reciprocate your desire, *to hope*.

The 7th: went to Meknes with Thami in the afternoon.

The dentist tells me that two Frenchmen were assassinated at El-Biar. I'm devastated.

[06/08/1995] The 8th.

To cope by having my life from you. Two letters reach me via Algeria. Masako writes on Good Friday, from her home: "It's my choice. I want to stay here. I've got the will to be rooted where I am. The Kingdom of God is here and now, not somewhere else. I celebrated twenty years in France with my friends. I left Japan in 1975 [. . .]. I feel something new is beginning this year. [. . .] I should very much like to contemplate God. I mean, I try to think more about God than about myself and to remain *under God's gaze*. He looks at me first, before I turn my eyes to him.

"You'll find some 'birds of freedom' enclosed. For my anniversary, I've given my friends 'birds of freedom' and tulip bulbs, symbolizing the seed planted."

Georgette wrote me from Syria on April 30, from Palmyra, then from Lebanon: "The idea is to launch a new example of inter-religious culture. I'm always available to return there [to Algeria]."

[06/09/1995] Friday 9th.

Ashura. "Liturgical" anniversary of my first monastic vows, 12-31-76 (Day of *Ashura* that year). From *La chambre nuptiale du cœur* ["The bridal chamber of the heart"],[23] the following excerpts:

From Saint Ephrem:[24]

> It is you, Lord, that they saw
> when they cast their glance at one another.
> It is you that your mother saw in your disciple
> and it is you that the disciple saw in your mother.
> It is you, Lord, that the Seers saw always, in a mirror.
> They proclaim that we, too,
> can see you, O you, our Savior,
> when we look at one another. (pp. 39–40)

And about the Samaritan woman:

> It is because she told him with desire:
> "The Messiah is coming"
> that he appeared to her with love: "I am he." (p. 41)

And from John of Dalyatha:[25]

> Look into yourself and see God within you.

23. Youakim Moubarac, *La chambre nuptiale du cœur : Approches spirituelles et questionnements de l'Orient syriani* (Paris: Cariscript, 1993); coll. Libanica, t. 4.

24. Ephrem the Syrian (ca. 306–373) was a deacon and a prolific Syriac-language hymnographer and theologian of the 4th century from the region of Syria.

25. Syrian mystic and spiritual writer of the 8th century. He is compared to Isaac of Nineveh, Saint John of the Cross, and Saint Thérèse of the Child Jesus.

Fasten your eyes on your heart and God, rising out of your heart, will shine on your soul.

If you look there continually, that is where you will find the Kingdom:

that is to say, you will find, in yourself, God, who is your kingdom.

Because their diligence, he reveals himself to the small number of those who keep their eyes fixed in their interior, making a mirror of themselves where the Invisible One can be seen. (p. 48)

From Macarius:[26]

When the soul has been enlightened, polished, made limpid and purified by the holy and adorable Spirit, we see limpidly, purely and clearly our true Friend, our Lord and our God, gentle and sweet, loved and cherished, our glorious Spouse, Christ the King [. . .] through the eyes of our intelligence. Then, also, it has become easy to contemplate, to see, to consider him, the Beautiful, in this resplendent, desirable, loved and beloved beauty, that is ineffable and incomprehensible.

Again, from John of Dalyatha:

Happy the one who in his soul has acquired the treasure of life which is Christ, who reveals himself to those who love him, for all riches are his.

Cover yourself with humility at all times, my friend, because it clothes your soul in the Christ who gives it to you. The shining star of beauty shall appear to the humble, rising above his heart, and at each genuflection he makes in prayer he shall see magnificent flashes.

Become a broom that is used for sweeping and a rag for wiping off all the dirt left by your brothers.

From Isaac:[27]

26. Saint Macarius of Egypt (ca. 300–391), Egyptian monk and hermit.
27. Isaac of Nineveh, or ("the Syrian"), 7th-century Assyrian bishop and theologian best remembered for his written work.

> When will a man know that his heart has attained purity? When he thinks that all men are good and that none of them is impure. It is at this moment that the heart of man is truly pure. And what is purity of heart? In short, it is the mercy that the heart experiences for the whole universe. [. . .] It is an unlimited compassion that is born in the heart of a man and makes him like God.

Simone Weil: "Distance is the soul of the beautiful" (*Gravity and Grace*).

On p. 96 [a picture of the Virgin]:

> Whether she is at the entrance to the sanctuary or at the heart of the assembly of disciples, the indwelling of the Spirit makes her as denuded and transparent as an empty niche. She points us in the direction of the Father and his presence, "toward the East."

On p. 105:

> Mission and contemplation. Henceforth, the pinnacle passes by way of the foundation. To teach presupposes that you speak the language of the one you want to instruct. But language cannot be separated from the culture it conveys, and there is no culture that is not fundamentally religious. To put "contemplation" as the foundation of a mission means that you want to bring about an encounter from the very beginning with those to whom you are sent, and to engage in a dialogue with them at the deepest level.

Teach . . . *go out* . . . The Church has not finished living this radical rupture of the mission, the way it is born of the verb "go out," with all that is involved in the sending of the 70 disciples, of whom it is demanded not even to bring a purse. Mission is radically liberated from the schema of colonization to the extent that "contemplation," the night of the senses and the heart, more than the detachment from one's own culture, bring about the encounter at the same point of rupture where the Spirit brings about its "conversion" in the very depth of every being and every people.

This understanding of mission-involvement in the workings of the Holy Spirit, thus the starting point of "contemplation," presupposes another understanding of God's design, where it is required of the "pagan" that he become a "Christian," or rather a "Judaeo-Christian." Barbarian → civilized; "to develop" the "under-developed": this is the colonial adventure.

As humble collaboration with the work of the two hands of the Father in the world and in history, mission is attention to this work, and the testimony given by its many burgeonings, which did not wait for the workers in order for the harvest to ripen in the field of the universe. Mission is compassion with the successive workings of decomposition and ripening that the Word and the Spirit make human generations pass through by means of the Paschal Mystery, which will only be revealed in all its aspects and for everybody at the Parousia.

From now until then, attention to the poorest is also a work of the same interior nature. It is he, Christ, mystically present in his suffering members, as "the Other" whom a Jean Vanier encounters in a painful and salutary manner in the handicapped. There too—especially there—mission and contemplation are but one.

> To be close is still to be too far; grace is still a part of wayfaring. The Lord is in me like an eternal possession!
>
> [. . .] He has sprung forth in me like roses on the hedgerows! I bloom in the red-thorn of His love, I bloom on all my branches in the purple of His gifts! [. . .] I bloom out of the Holy Spirit of the Lord. (Gertrud von Le Fort,[28] *Hymns to the Church)*

At the Eucharist every day we are reading the Book of Tobit. Yesterday, the son brought the remedy that he got from the Angel to cure his father's diseased eyes. The son cured his father. Then his father embraced him and wept: "I see you, my son, light of

28. Gertrud von Le Fort (1876–1971) was a noted German Catholic convert and writer of novels, poems, and essays with religious themes.

my eyes!" Paternity is a matter of seeing. The Angel had said these words of Hope on God's behalf: "I know that his eyes will be opened."

Thus, one who accompanies a brother should enter into this "knowledge of hope," seeing beyond difficulties, blockages and various birth pangs.

How to settle one's account with Raphael? To "repay God" is meaningless. Jesus in the Temple reveals the nothingness of money, which has no value except when it *is given* in truth: the poor widow has really given her two small coins. To celebrate the Eucharist draws us into the offering of the Poor: living and holy.

[06/11/1995] Sunday. HOLY TRINITY.

Happiness arrives for me. LOVE that chases all fear from my heart. No, I am sure of it: HOPE does not deceive. Your life cannot lie.

"The unknown and the marvels of God do not so much have to be defined as discovered and lived in the daily hope of exchange and communion, mutual respect and transcendence, dialogue and community, in a unity that is realized in differences, in all love that opens up rather than shuts down, that creates and multiplies rather than holds back jealously" (F.D.).

> Once he has ascended all the degrees of humility, the monk will quickly arrive at the love of God, which casts out all fear because it is perfect. Through it, all that he observed in the beginning, not without anxiety, he begins to observe without effort, as if naturally and by habit, no longer out of fear of gehenna, but out of the love of Christ, by acquired habit and the joy of virtue. THIS is what the Lord will deign to manifest, by the HOLY SPIRIT, in his laborer, now purified of his vices and sins. (*Rule of Saint Benedict,* 7.67-70)

Note: "A Trinitarian conclusion: the monk's way to God does not only imply moral perfection, but also ontological completion (I am—deification) in the love of God the Father, through the love of Christ his Son, in the grace of the Holy Spirit." (Dom Herwegen)[29]

Meeting with X., who broaches with courage and great frankness "a delicate and unavoidable question": his relationship with me is difficult for him: "a source of discomfort, leaving a bad taste and causing blockage and shutdown. I feel threatened, ill at ease, no affinity between us, not an atom of real contact already at Tibhirine." Then follows an analysis of his situation as a novice on the basis of a word "that I don't like and you often use: *stakes*" (at Tibhirine: the humiliation of the ego). Here F.L. is called in as reinforcement. "All of you have *staked* so much on me here that it's too heavy a burden for my shoulders: preparing for my arrival / the story of the novices who came before me / prayer in the novitiate with the community."

And then I hear also that my interventions have turned out badly as regards organizing his personal schedule (for instance, the trip to the Little Sisters in Rabat), and that at N. things are different, more flexible. I restate the question of a temporary engagement at Atlas and what it means, in comparison with the other possibility: to make vows at N., which would receive X., and the call that he strongly feels to come and join the Atlas community.

I notice again something in myself that seems to get "to the bottom of things"—and I said it to X.: "I sense a wound in you that awakens my own wound and makes me feel insecure."

What did I answer to all this? We need to redefine our relationship, since it is not a goal in itself. The stakes (!) for relationships are high in a small community [. . .]. Neither one of us should give up, hoping it is possible to move beyond all this by accepting one other, including our wounds.

I make X. a gift of one of the two *"birds of freedom"* I got from Masako.

29. Ildefons Herwegen (1874–1946), German Benedictine monk, abbot of Maria Laach, church historian and liturgist, author of a commentary on the Rule of Saint Benedict: *Sinn und Geist der Benediktinerregel* (Einsiedeln: Benziger Verlag, 1944).

Is X. able to take on the "stake" of a monastic engagement at Tibhirine in Algeria, even at a distance? Aren't we rather moving toward a "non-binding" stay in October: a reconciliation visit—without vows?

Father Pierre whispers to me: Those who truly seek God have experienced the terrible torture involved in a conversion of heart to Love that is pursued unflinchingly.

I have to hold on for another two weeks. Yes, I've just written this. But, after a good meeting with Father Jean, the stronger reality is that for X. all of this is positive and good. And it makes me painfully happy. As for the demands on my part that may seem exaggerated to him, simply "too much," I cannot give them up, they are a part of your call: to follow you on the way of the Gospel, at Our Lady of Atlas, in Algeria.

I talk on the phone with Mom and Dad tonight.

[06/12/1995] Monday.

YOUR WORD is a lamp to my feet. Last night, before I fell asleep, I read: "I say to you, my friends, *fear not* those who kill the body, after that they can do nothing." You really do show me the direction, the decisive orientation that mobilizes my weakness, yes, you call me to live at Tibhirine to the end.

Father, near Her, I say to you again
in Jesus: here I am
Spirit of Love guide my steps
on the road of humility.

Today, on the mountain, grace and truth overtake the law, fulfilled as grace: Oh, happiness.

"Happy the poor of spirit for theirs is the Kingdom of heaven; happy the pure hearts for they shall see God" [in Arabic in the text: *tûbâ lifuqarâ' al-rûkh înâ lakhum malakût al-samawât—tûba li'athari al-qulûb fainnâkhum yushâhidûm Allah*]. And then the Apostle (2 Cor 1:3-4): "*Blessed be God*, the Father of our Lord Jesus Christ, the Father of mercies and the God of all consolation, who consoles us so that we may be able to console."

May my hope as regards X. remain *firm*, Lord: happy are the pure in heart, they shall see you.

[06/14/1995] Wednesday 14th.

Thanks to You, everything went well. We came back from Taza just in time for Vespers, rich with the encounters You gave us to live together: opening up to one another when our relationship was (is) running the risk of shutting down, of being blocked. We were with the sisters: Anne-Marie, Denise, Maria (from Portugal) and Irenia (from Poland). With Nureddin Monday evening. In the morning with Naima, Rabia (Sophiane), and, before leaving, her husband Amin.

[06/16/1995] Friday.

I am counting the days. My presence here has become heavy. While Guy is away, I am in charge of Nejma. I feed her, and we are good friends. Her affection is touching. Just like that!

The mail is spoiling me with sweet and encouraging letters: Ileana ("I know it's a funny thing to say to a monk, but I'd love to see you"). Dad and Mom. Zabeth. Brother Yann.

[06/17/1995] My sweetness: sweet Mary.

[06/18/1995] Sunday. Corpus Christi.

Jesus welcomes (the crowds), he speaks of the Kingdom of God, he heals (me).

Lord, subject the Enemy in me all the way to my heart
be between X. and me like the dew that is born of the
    dawn
  teach me to keep nothing back
  from your surrendered life
  I receive you: my life
  you my joy, my cry
  oh, give yourself in me.

To understand
the hunger of the other

and believe that you,
risen Jesus, using what I bring you
(no matter how disproportionate that might be
to the expectations of this other
who at bottom hungers for love—word and healing)
you are going to respond
and I shall be but the servant of the GIFT
simply
lovingly.

A encounter of you with X.
right in our midst—
will this be possible?
I would like to be available, receptive,
without imposing anything
I would love to be able to give thanks with X.
for so many beautiful things received
true miracles
that multiply life
and makes it overflow
there is always life left over
for your love is eternal.

There's the return here to Morocco, where his vocation was born, and undoubtedly other things
there's the community of Fez welcoming him,
there was—as far as he and I are concerned—our first meeting just before Vigils, and Marc was there.

The problems only came later: let's not let them drown out those moments of simple fraternity
there is the "light" *kora*, the chanting,
there is A. and the Arabic language
there was Taza.

Thank you: you granted
that we should meet
in Spirit
in Truth.

[06/19/1995] Monday.

In solitude until the Eucharist (in the parish) this evening.

In thanksgiving (with Douce—the Sweet One) [in Arabic in the text: *wa dî 'atî wa dî 'atî huluâ*].

At the meal yesterday: Father Voillaume,[30] greatness and the strength of a founder who identifies himself with the history of the fraternities. I should have loved to sense his detachment. Like Jesus himself: "I go away, I come to you."

2 Cor 6:1-10. See, you offer me this day. I receive it from your hand,

behold, now is a very acceptable time;

behold, now is my day of salvation: by your Joy, Father,

ah, deliver me from laziness (a disobedience that is flight, self-concealment, weakness), let me not make your GRACE to be without effect.

I remember the day when your GRACE, leaning on my poverty, made me your priest,
a minister of You, Love.

And I did not know it. And I'd like to live up to your desire, to your thirst to give the Gift to all.

Make me to the utmost
the servant of your *I love you.*
Nothing else attracts me by way of
greatness or honor.
I want so much to let myself be led
all the way to this abyss of inaccessible
humility—that attracts me.
Such happiness has become
necessary, vital.
Today, HOLY SPIRIT,
hold me, gather me up

30. René Vouillaume (1906–2003), founder of the congregation of the Little Brothers of Jesus (Paris, 1933), inspired by the life and writings of Blessed Charles de Foucauld. The first contemplative monastic fraternity was founded in the Sahara, in southern Algeria.

in truth: in Christ my Lord.
Let my life—flesh and blood
and tears and song—
say whatever you say.
Holy Father, I know it: you listen to me,
your Love awakens
my child's voice.
Near Her: here I am.

great perseverance (constancy)
in all forms of distress
    constraints   all sorts of anguish
    beatings   prisons
    riots   constant fatigue
    vigils   fasts
Purity
Knowledge
Patience   HOLY SPIRIT
Goodness
    unfeigned love
    words of truth
    power of God
offensive arms
  defensive for justice
in glory and contempt,
in bad and good reputation
regarded as impostors, yet speaking the truth
unknown and yet well known.
Dying and yet
we live.

Punished but not executed
saddened, but always joyful
poor yet enriching many
having nothing, and yet we possess everything.

Out of the open book You make me a gift of these burning, vibrant words:

Jn 7:38-39. "If any man is thirsty, let him come to me and drink, he who believes in me. As scripture says: 'From his breast shall flow fountains of living water.'"

He was speaking of the SPIRIT that those who would believe in him were to receive, for there was no SPIRIT yet
because JESUS had not yet been glorified.
to live
happens to me river
simply your life
poured out heart to heart
and gently too
to die
is necessary
in order to
see
gently being born to your gaze
a heart bowed simply to thank you
without end
praise you
In your *I am* Jesus
I am, wholly in Love
like Her (a little bit, so little . . .)
through her—my Sweetheart—offered up
(passionately)
near her committed (in your madness)
your Cross assigns us (on the mountain)
as victims? victors for being
divinely beloved
Jesus
savior of the world
come quickly
our world is dying
of not believing in You.

I finished the *Revelations* [*of Divine Love,* by Julian of Norwich]. I have found a friend. You had arranged our meeting here in Fez. Thank you!

[. . .]

Today you tell me not to resist the wicked, not on his own ground (violence, lies, hatred). On the contrary, if anyone strikes you on the right cheek, turn the other as well.

Do not renounce your dignity, your highest and most vulnerable truth: your face engages me in this battle. The stronger Love: "I am with you."

In the *Petit traité des grandes vertus* ["A Small Treatise on the Great Virtues"], by André Comte-Sponville,[31] I am finishing the 17th virtue: humor. Then comes the last chapter: love.

In order to turn the other cheek to one who strikes me, first I must know . . . where it is;

I must have experienced the actual fact that another cheek exists.

Jesus, it seems to me I'm [in the process of] learning this.

Love, it is you who reveal to me that other cheek—my best profile—the one that belongs to eternity, and it will be the only one without any possible duplicity or ambivalence. The other cheek: my profile of hope.

May I contemplate it in every man and woman.
It is yourself on the face of every living person.
It is the other cheek that a kiss reveals,
my face of light
that your gaze illumines.

[06/20/1995] The 20th.

At the kiss of peace, Jesus, you offered me your beautiful smile on X.'s face.

My gaze is overwhelmed by this.
You show me that I can be, that I am
gentle
because you are gentle [in Arabic in the text: *faînna anta wadî'*].

31. André Comte-Sponville (b. 1952), French philosopher, a proponent of atheism and materialism but in a particular form, because of his spiritualistic aim. He intends to overcome traditional materialistic atheism in a perspective of post-materialism, because he seeks to work out a spiritualization of atheism. *A Small Treatise on the Great Virtues* (1995; tr. Catherine Temerson, Vintage, 2003).

[06/21/1995] Wednesday.

Yesterday afternoon: In the Medina with Thami to buy a few things. Thank you, Lord, for simple men.

Today, Saint Louis Gonzaga, a young man who is pure and holy.

Since I haven't got the same innocence, at least, Lord, I can hope and allow myself to be purified by You: Love.

As regards X.: detachment; my "disinterest" should remain a love that is detached, disinterested, freely given.

I cannot relinquish this charge

because one day I received the mission of being father-master. The title doesn't matter.

May your secret gaze, Father, keep me faithful: a servant and a friend.

[06/22/1995] Thursday.

2 Co 11:2. "I betrothed you to one husband to present you as a chaste virgin to Christ. But I am afraid that, as the serpent deceived Eve by his cunning, your thoughts may be corrupted far from the SIMPLICITY due to Christ."

Little Sisters Françoise, Raymonde, Meriem, José and Franca.

Must (re-)read *The Art of the Icon*, by Paul Evdokimov.

[06/23/1995] Friday.

I shall drink from the wellspring of your ♡.

Yes, you have come, my beautiful shepherd with the wounded heart,

you have come all the way to me, a lost sheep, and you've taken me up on your shoulders.

In you I go forward: make me docile to all the movements of your heart until the very last one.

Father John of the Cross makes reference to the hymn of Saint Symeon the New Theologian, about joy and courage through tears.

Couscous with Thami.

A unique thing in the Order, says Father John of the Cross.

Two delightful meetings in the afternoon: with Father John of the Cross, then with Father Jean-Baptiste, who says: "I am most a priest at the end of the Canon ('Through Him and with Him and in Him'), so that the prayer of the Muslims may be united to Christ's. After the Council, I thought to myself that a laybrother could be ordained a priest while remaining faithful to the spirit of the laybrothers."

[06/24/1995] Saturday 24th.

Birth of John the Baptist. (Immaculate Heart of Mary.)

[06/27/1995] Tuesday 27th.

At Tibhirine since yesterday, arriving for Vespers and Eucharist.

[06/29/1995] June 29th.

Saints Peter and Paul.

[07/11/1995] July 11th.

BENEDICT of Jesus Christ. Must use this day to get a fresh hold on the holy and noble weapons of obedience, to leave free play in me to the Spirit of the PEACE of Christ. Father, here I am: fulfill in me the commitment we have undertaken here. Why haven't I written anything since I came back from Fez? No doubt I've been caught up in life here, which is so demanding. You can't turn your back on such urgent calls. Living is truly the task here. Our community seems to me to be (still) quite alive, even within the affliction suffered by one of us, who is a suffering servant in the midst of a suffering people. But even so, the community is tired: the load we carry goes beyond our poor strength, which is in decline. I needed to forget Fez and the wound discovered there. Yesterday, a "difficulty in relationship" again made me feel low and upset. I don't handle it well. Violence knocks me out, and I need to find a support somewhere so I don't let myself be dragged off by this tide of death. What's the good of making my presence felt if my existence disturbs others, impinges on others, and asserts itself to their detriment?

Kenosis is the only model of fraternal existence, on condition that it be infinitely, resolutely, wildly filial: the happiness of a poor man who does not wrong anyone. No doubt it is better to keep such happiness *hidden*—and allow myself quite simply to be consumed by it. If You want to give others something coming from me, I trust you with that. I'll let you choose, whether it's the least bad in me or the best, which only your gaze can awaken, draw forth and harvest at the proper time.

[07/13/1995] Thursday 13th.

It's our bishop's feast day. He came to celebrate Saint Benedict's with us. A simple and wonderful meeting yesterday with Little Sister Marie Charlotte, who is fragile and at the same time so strong, so "indwelt." To open up, one to the other, is to recognize you. Separation intervenes so quickly! Something took place between her and me, a living relationship that "hurts" me (and this is the Good coming from your wounded and open heart).

[07/14/1995] The 14th.

Simone Weil: "There are two forms of friendship: encounter and separation. They are inseparable. Both of them contain the same good, the only good, friendship. For, when two beings who are not friends are close, there is no encounter. When they are far apart, there is no separation. Since both contain the same good, they are equally good" *(Waiting for God*, p. 132). A monk is someone who is *separated* from everyone *and united* to everyone. It is a question of friendship. "This love, this friendship in God, is the Trinity. Between the terms that are united in this relationship of divine love, there is more than proximity; there is infinite proximity, identity. But through Creation, Incarnation and Passion there is also an infinite distance. The totality of space, the totality of time, interposing their 'density', put an infinite distance between God and God" (*idem*).

[07/15/1995] Saturday.

More "difficulties of relationship." This evening I read Jean Vanier (*Toute personne est une histoire sacrée* ["Every Person Is a Sacred History"]): "In order to truly find full communion with God [and with the others], I know that one must descend to the bottom of the abyss in order to ascend even more alive."

[07/16/1995] Sunday.

I need this Day that belongs to You. Make me over, I am falling apart. The meeting with Christian this morning was good. There is something of you in his listening, in his words, in his gaze, in his closeness. An encouragement to say "I" in the relationship. It's also the story of the Good Samaritan.

[07/19/1995] Wednesday.

I was saying to Christian: "The best thing one can offer to another is his freedom," which can be received only within a relationship that is freeing. Then the difficulty of my existence, this problem gnawing at me, is clearly seen: how to say "I" without doing violence to anybody? Perhaps one must first renounce—gradually—all self-assertion that doesn't occur within a relationship to another. I certainly still experience occasions of violent self-assertion in a given relationship. This remains a vital force; but I must keep the impulse while converting its power so as to offer it to the other. I am pure

I am in order to offer you the occasion of being you
I shall not evade it
I am here to be-with.

[07/21/1995] Friday 21st.

Jean Vanier: "A weak person leads us toward what is deepest in ourselves" (p. 219).

[07/23/1995] Sunday.

I am reader. I'm sure I heard Saint Bruno of (?) say that the contemplative life *has no home.* It's a matter of being present for the only thing to be lived for: the relationship. So what do I hear about You here at Tibhirine? For two days, Fire has spoken to us. It got close to the school. And, like your disciples in the garden, I was asleep: siesta obliges. Did I wake up? The disciple who is born on the Cross ("Behold your son!") is standing upright for the one thing necessary, joined to you for this final thing that is beyond me.

Last night I was storm-tossed, agitated, whirled about, like Martha's way of serving. Did it come from hearing Christian talk to us about Camille (what Gospel power in this letter, when I heard it again!), and even more about X., who had written to him. He continues at N. Monastic life might almost appear to be a cause—a just and good one!—to which one might well sacrifice everything. It would seem we belong to something imaginary?

Long live the reality of N., and death to Atlas![32]

I know, just the same, that a subject is about to be born.

"If you knew the Gift."

To become the subject of the verb "to give"—"no greater love . . ."—there is no other way than relationship. But the relationship with You, the Crucified, leads to the knowledge of the Gift that will come as the Cross, as suffering. How shall I hold out if I do not hold on to you: you give me your LIFE that I may live to the point of dying, if necessary.

It seems to me that one needs to keep watch over the person's full freedom in the face of this adventure of the gift today, in Algeria.

On pp. 152–53, Simone Weil writes: "To desire the existence of this faculty of free consent in another person who has been deprived of it by some misfortune, means for one to move into

32. Brother Christophe is clearly being ironical in this passage as he records X.'s antithetical views of the two communities of N. and Atlas (i.e., Tibhirine).

the other, to consent to this misfortune in oneself, that is, to consent to one's own destruction. It means to deny oneself. By denying oneself one becomes capable, after God, of affirming another through a creative affirmation. One gives oneself as ransom for the other. It is an act of redemption."

[07/25/1995] July 25th. A feast in the ♡.

On this day I ask you for the grace to become a servant
and to give my life
here
as a ransom for PEACE
as a ransom for LIFE
Jesus draw me
into your joy
of crucified love.

W. spoke to us at chapter last night with moving truth. I entrust him to Christian Chessel.

The day after the feast. The true feast—the feast of the other (James), of the Other

that the voice of the Father points out: This is
my Son
—my feast
—listen to
him

So many signs of You on this 25th of July:

In the mail: from Japan (M.), from Ancône (Mom's suffering over Dad being bedridden), from Talence (B.) and Tamié (D.). A meal with music, delicious sherbet . . . books . . . Eucharist and fatigue at the end of the day. Christian: God has ambitions for each one of us.

[07/30/1995] Sunday.

You—at prayer: teach us here to be like YOU.

Yes, here, a place W. is going to forsake. For what other tie(s)? Yesterday, before Lauds, I received the light from these words of yours: "Every branch that bears fruit, he (your Father) prunes so that it may bear even more." Even more: what do you mean by that for us here? . . . To love like you.

[07/31/1995] Monday.

A day arrives when you receive an impulse that makes you flee the world and go through a door. "What do you ask for?"[33] When there is nothing more to ask for, there's nothing left but to flee from the monastery. This is what's happening before our very eyes today: a plunging toward death. We are witnessing this rush toward a lie. As Moussa says: "For us, there is no choice." We must pray for W.

Yesterday on the phone Mom told me that—despite her suffering over the fact that she and Dad can barely communicate—she is able to pray an Our Father and a Hail Mary with him every day, hands joined: I want to slip into this poor and naked adoration of theirs.

[08/01/1995] Tuesday.

No: W., almost in tears during Eucharist, received the grace to get access to what he is missing, to the question: "Do You love me?" We have simply made room for Your Response. The community is that "we" that gives you birth. But we are all quite exhausted. For several days, Christian is obsessed with a question: "Fez?" His mother is in a clinic after a fall yesterday. You are trying us . . . and we are far from being worth one ounce of gold.

[08/13/1995] Sunday 13th.

Célestin is in the hospital in Medea. The trees have been cut down.

33. "What do you ask for?" is the ritual question asked of a novice on entering the monastery.

[08/15/1995] August 15th.

Mary rises and leaves in haste. A dream last night: I was digging a grave. I heard from Kh. yesterday: that Brother Luc was going to leave (!!?). No. On the phone I had Mom, then Dad. Coming down from the vineyard, I meet Mohammed Q. B. and his young son on the road. We greet each other with "Peace!" He says: "There are always those who sacrifice themselves. There is always suffering." He's taking his son to the hospital.

[08/18/1995] Friday.

Yesterday we went with Michel to see Célestin in the hospital, one sick person among other sick persons, in a sick country. He's well cared for, respected, visited, loved, but still living on the brink of depression. Christian showed me a letter from John of the Cross: "an immense fatigue. . . ." Where will this take him? I remember the "bird of freedom" that I gave him in Fez.

"He who made his way to us from the Father makes himself our way by his Palestinian endeavor" (J. Grosjean). Yes, you † are our only emergency way out: come quickly.

[08/20/1995] August 20th.

Saint Bernard: your day. Let us be happy! This is our claim to glory: we are those to whom God pays attention. *Sermon on the Song of Songs 67.* Jean-Bernard is at Tamié, which is so far away.

[08/22/1995] Tuesday.

All right! It's useless trying to count us (we are one more with Célestin, coming back from the hospital today). You've shown me that we total 144,000, and that a new song arises from this countless body of humanity.

[08/23/1995] Wednesday.

I don't think anyone among us is much concerned with his own life. This greatly clears the way before us as a community!

[08/25/1995] Friday.

Last night, a big squall in choir at Vespers! You know that I long for the new Song. And no one has been able to learn that song, except the 144,000 who have been redeemed from the world. Those whom God, by his Christ, has made his own, and their soul is a new melody: infused, inalienable, nascent, dawning, filial (J. Grosjean, *Apocalypse*, p. 77).

They follow the Lamb wherever he goes.

You can make it so that I can accompany my father and mother in these painful days,

without ceasing to walk here in your mad and sweet Presence.

[08/26/1995] Saturday.

To give voice does not mean to brandish one's voice like a victorious weapon, sweeping away everything around one. But I ought not to keep my voice back for myself. One finds it by losing it. To give one's voice is an illusion if You, Lord, don't receive it.

At bottom, my voice is but a single cry: Come quickly.

[08/27/1995] Sunday.

Stormy chapter. As cantor still on duty, I am (painfully) at the epicenter of the mini-earthquake. I'm shaken up.

A dream last night. It was here. Christian and I are in the garden. A noise makes us look up. It's a helicopter. It lands. The officer who climbs out—smiling broadly—offers to take my mother with him. She's on a stretcher. It's difficult to lift her into it because various incidents interfere. Father is worried about what will happen to her. Finally, both of them are lifted up.

What I heard yesterday made me re-live a situation of rejection that is identical to the one I experienced with X. (So it seems to me, but the rejection may just stem from my own psychological state.) He was saying to me: "Back off!," and then repeated it more politely afterwards. I got it: "Shut up! We've had enough of you." I'm going to thank Christian and ask him not to give me any more support. It's a lost cause. I lack humility. And hope is rare nowadays.

Could I be going through the "narrow gate," on my way toward an inaccessible "elsewhere"? Please, don't let go of me. Out of the depths I cry.

[08/30/1995] Wednesday.

I am reading Qoheleth, who invites me to live what I receive from You. Hope can only start from embracing something real whose ulterior evolution I do not know, nor can I penetrate its secret. "We must have humor," Christian said to me in connection with the singing on Sunday: "A joyful disappointment."

[08/31/1995] Thursday.

I must remember this word—*sáhªra* [literally, "desert"]—repeated frequently by our neighbors when looking at the landscape that was massacred by the chain saw (and the bulldozer, near the vineyard). Yes, we are led into the desert. It's a confirmation of our vocation. Yesterday a touching letter to listen to: in it, Father Elred of Kasanza[34] speaks about Camille.

If it is right to resist the violence that dehumanizes both faces and landscapes, there's also something to accept that we've been given to LIVE. Here even joy may happen: you!

[09/01/1995] Friday.

In Sarajevo you can get killed just by going out shopping. At Bab el-Oued yesterday it was a booby-trapped car that killed people. And I am still alive. By what right? For what responsibility as a survivor? Qoheleth says that there is hope for whoever is bound to all the living (9:4). That is what happens to every disciple at the foot of the cross: to be with Mary in the communion of the living, in the bond of LIFE with YOU, crucified Love.

34. Kasanza: Our Lady of the Emmanuel, a Cistercian monastery of brothers near Kikwit, in the Democratic Republic of Congo.

[09/02/1995] Saturday.

I was moved reading a letter from Tamié brought back by Gilles. The one writing me is close to me—Jean-Marie, embracing his life as the most wonderful reprieve. Yes, brother, you're right: we're being reprieved for the moment. There is a closeness among those who are reprieved. Being here in Algeria does not dispense me from being with you, and with my father on his sickbed.

Julian of Norwich: "I saw partially the compassion of the blessed lady saint Mary. She was one with Christ in love. The greatness of her love was the cause of the greatness of her suffering."

[09/04/1995] Monday 4th.

During the night, before the beginning of Vigils, Christian announced to us that two of our sisters, Vivianne and Angela, were assassinated this Sunday evening at Belcourt coming out of Mass. I read and re-read the Apocalypse. Forward, reader! Yes, it's all about You, the victorious Lamb who is slain. About You, who are coming quickly. And I should like to be caught up in your Movement of LIFE given away. Vivianne and Angela: the Unveiling of Jesus Christ here. It's with your testimony that they've testified. A journalist (the 39th) was also assassinated: only he is mentioned in the news bulletin on Algiers Channel III.

[09/05/1995] Tuesday.

The announcement during the night continues to speak to me: the Unveiling of Jesus Christ, a revelation of You. "Two of our sisters, Vivianne and Angela . . . ," Christian said; he must hardly have slept. Yes, two from among our sisters, more specifically sisters in crucified Love.

[09/15/1995] Friday 15th.

Standing near the Cross, the mother and, near her, the beloved disciple. At the Maison Saint-Augustin, where I stayed two days, I heard these words from a sister and a priest: "I don't know." — "Oh, I don't know any more. . . ." Indeed, that's where we are as a Church, stripped of all knowing perspective. But aren't we experiencing another kind of knowledge: a Christ-like understanding of the situation, a lowly (Marian) way of thinking?

I came back with a "word of life" received from Thomas Merton. The monk, he says, does not exist in order to preserve anything at all, not even contemplation, not even religion. [. . .] On the contrary, the function of the monk of our time is TO KEEP HIMSELF ALIVE THROUGH HIS CONTACT WITH GOD.

[09/18/1995] Monday 18th.

". . . and HOPE does not disappoint, because the love of God has been poured out into our hearts through the Holy Spirit that has been given to us" (Rom 5:5). You: Love, pure Hope, Holy Father.

[09/19/1995] Tuesday.

I am witness to a beautiful detachment: I see it in Célestin, I see it in Jean-Pierre, and I see it in each one of us. Someone is drawing us to himself. A preference obliges us.

[09/30/1995] Saturday 30th.

Like an image of the whole country, our vineyard has failed. The best thing would be to tear it up and try growing something else. Ben Sirach says to me: "Be faithful to your task and put your joy into it" (or "ponder it," with A. Chouraqui), and grow old in your work. Again, I feel wobbly in my office as cantor. I think less and less of it. Give way to the scribes! I fill a place unduly. I'm still far from letting myself be stripped of my powers.

[10/02/1995] Monday 2nd.

Little Thérèse, I beg you, do me some good so that I won't do something wrong (such as my occupation as monk here). I read the words of Qoheleth: "Onwards (or 'happy') the man who is never deceived by his whole being, and whose hope never stands idle" (14:2).

[10/03/1995] Tuesday.

A letter from Philippe [of Tamié] arrived yesterday. You know when to give me needed provisions that are as surprising as they're substantial. I give you thanks. I feel I'm being taken in hand again. I'm going to try to let go of controls, to let myself go wherever you want. A fax from Zaire is waiting for us in Algiers. The violence never stops. More than ever now—when a bulldozer is massacring the forest at the army's command (close to Lalla Meriem: Our Lady of Compassion)—we're being asked to become those "trees that exist silently in the dark and by their vital presence purify the air" (Thomas Merton).

[10/04/1995] Wednesday.

Saint Francis—the Poverello. I'd really love it if one day my life would sing in unison with yours, in the joy of wounded Love. Mary, you who know all the saints one by one: could you tighten my bond with your child from Assisi? I would make him my singing teacher. My objective: to arrive at my 45th birthday in your company. And (?) to entrust to you all that is to follow—resolutely, recklessly.

[10/20/1995] 10/20.

Since the 3rd quite a few things have happened to me. First, my Dad. He died on October 5th around 10 p.m. I had arrived in Ancône at 5.30 p.m. I returned to Algiers on the 16th, changed by having lived through my father's death. Maybe I lived it like a baptism. Don't we say: "Baptized in Christ's death, we shall live with him"? I looked at his suffering face, which was looking for the Breath of life as never before. I contemplated my father as he was being led by the Spirit to his whole truth. I am not fixated on one image that grips me. This is a loved face, one infinitely gazed upon. This face awaits me. Jesus' Last Supper already gives us a place where we exchange glances. Mine is a look of faith, hope, and charity; yours is invaded by Love.

[10/21/1995] Saturday 10/21.

While at Ancône I rounded 45 years. I must live according to You: here, *I love you.* I felt the force of that *I must* a few days before taking the plane at Satolas (Lyon), and just when I arrived at the airport: "Possible return at 1200 meters"! And I didn't feel the need to discern. I clung to a movement (as the Father has sent me, I also you, I . . . you). This Thursday I presided at the Eucharist for Dad's intention: "Pierre, your servant." I remembered my prayer at his side as he was dying, as he was living his death. My prayer was to you, dying on the cross (and there we were very close to you, whom we recognized in him): "Jesus, remember him, take him with you, today, into your Kingdom." And it was the evening of Yom Kippur: the great pardon, the one given by the greatest love. Mother had received this last message from Dad: "Tell Christophe that I have doubted much yet always believed."

I said after the gospel that I saw myself as heir to such a faith, permeated and thoroughly kneaded by doubt. It only remains for me to believe until the end. The doubts that assail me are not those of my father, but rather concern Hope. It was good for me to be able to say "in public" these words of Jesus in the gospel: "You are Peter and on this rock I will build my Church." They cannot be reserved for our Pope exclusively. Doesn't Jesus here want to make us understand—and Peter first of all—that his Church is not founded on ideas (so often murderous . . . in the end), but on the existence of believers—not without the trials of doubt—but believers until the end?

Dad! Now you are discovering the Church. You are happy to *belong* to her ("I'm not one of them," Peter said by the fire): beloved in the Communion of the Beloved. Help your human family, too, to discover this mystery.

[10/27/1995] Friday 27th.

"Happy the man whose fault is taken away, whose sin is forgiven." Yes, I know that this man is happy with you. I wrote to Mom about my joy at knowing them—her and Dad—to be profoundly united. I believe also that death and suffering allowed Dad to enter into a more complete freedom: to love even more. Jesus: thank you for drawing us, too, into your Free obedience.

[10/29/1995] Sunday.

Christ is risen.

In the issue of *Liturgie* (no. 94) that arrived yesterday I read: "With absolute realism and admirable clear-sightedness, the wise man in Psalm 48 looked death in the face. He saw that death, for man, is the test of total dispossession: sounding the defeat of all possessions, it tears away the illusion of having anything, in order to unveil to him the abyss of Being. The psalmist's faith and hope permit him, nevertheless, to say more, to reveal, in a flash of lightning, the secret of a certain 'being-with': the being-with a God who redeems man, the being-with a Love that is stronger than death. [Note 8: This is the promise the dying Jesus makes the good thief: 'Truly, I say to you, today you shall be with me in paradise.'] ['But God will ransom me from the claws of death, and take me to himself', Ps 48:16]." (Sister Étienne R., pp. 207–8)

And on p. 217, Henri Couleau writes: "Meaning is beyond the subject. If it is a question of celebrating this subject, the celebration consists in situating it, understanding it, within a myth or a mystery that signifies it" (see 11/1 attached here: J. Sommet,[35] quoted in my homily).

[11/02/1995] November 2nd.

Remembering our departed.

35. Jacques Sommet (1912–2012), French Jesuit priest and author, deported to Dachau during World War II.

[11/05/1995] The 5th. Sunday.

Yesterday, the assassination of the prime minister in Tel Aviv. Last night, after Vigils, my thoughts returned, as they often do these days, to the event of Dad's death (no news either from Mom or anyone else in the family). I wrote: Almighty God, yes, almighty precisely there on your face disfigured by pain, almighty before the enemy who is finishing you off. In order to win he chooses to wed your extreme misery. He puts on your agony and breathes his Spirit into your exhausted life. Love surrendered, strong as death.

[11/06/1995] The 6th.

With my eyes, on your bed, I have seen you
Love that is suffering, struggling
I have seen you vanquish death—from the inside—with a
naked face—
When his time came, you took him, Pierre your servant
baptized into your death
to take him with you—risen for us
into your completion: his filial truth.
I did not see it
my eyes impressed gripped
don't return from there. Joy.

[11/07/1995] The 7th.

Kneeling beside Mom who held your hand, so poor

I saw You in that bond. I held out my hand to be nourished by it.

Back at Tibhirine, I wrote to Mom: "My Joy was to see you two so profoundly united."

I could feel You move: You bowed down leaning over Dad: This one is my son, my beloved. Our recovery was then accomplished by small strokes of the brush. Singing. Alleluia. More prayers, sleeping and getting up again, extending welcome, leaning on one another, comforting one another, listening to one other. Celebrating Your day: Sunday is not a day for funerals. The inert body, hidden from our eyes (but not from Yours) stayed in the church for a long while (thanksgiving, act of contrition: yes, gratitude: Mercy!). A short visit at the end of the afternoon. And then on Monday, it was transferred to the place of his childhood. Blois. La Vrillière. Micheline, Jean, Evelyne were there. The cemetery of Saint-Lubin. Then the burial: an act of trust that strips the soul and lays it bare. No one fell into the grave. We supported one another, and there was You among us, sustaining us all. We walked away from the cemetery, and then gathered again.

[11/08/1995] The 8th.

When I arrived at Ancône, I was brought into the Presence. I entered the luminous cloud, introduced there by you, Mom, and you, Élisabeth. You were so truly present there: the wife and the daughter. What was my place? A son returning from afar, but also the monk-priest about whom, Dad, you had written me something like this: "After your ordination, I'll have nothing more to wait for: I can die."

I was at once placed beside the transfixed woman: as beloved disciple.

I saw you, Mom, to one side, in the shadow—not of your husband but of the Spirit.

I saw you covered by shadow, dressed in sweetness, in tenderness, in humility. You were talking to him about the other world. You alone could do that in truth. You finally attained the word you had to speak to him: a word of comfort and companionship

you came together again

and Bertrand was there also: three of the twelve. Why those three?

Françoise arrived at last—"another daughter," Mom said—another woman.

This morning, I say to myself that now—I am definitely born: I am grown-up enough to live and die with You.

Nothing remains but to stay alive thanks to You
until you come.
O come.

After Terce, Christian announced the deaths of Sister Odette and Sister Chantal, Little Sisters of the Sacred Heart: assassinated in their own neighborhood. For "others" to become an oblation sanctified by the Spirit, pleasing to God, there is no other means except offering oneself in You, with You, through You. Chantal is only wounded.

[11/12/1995] Sunday.

Children of the Resurrection. Coheirs of the Living One. Arise then, my love, my lovely one, go forth to encounter yourself. For see, winter is past: such is Odette on this 10th of November, 1995.

[11/13/1995] Monday 11/13.

Day of All monastic Saints and Forty Days' remembrance [for Dad]. Mom and Malika will pray together. In Algiers this morning: Eucharist and burial of Sister Odette. I haven't forgotten that beautiful dream one night during Lent when, turning around during a very solemn procession in front of Sacré-Cœur Cathedral, I saw you, Odette, dressed in priestly vestments, standing next to me as fellow concelebrant, wearing the green chasuble of Ordinary Time! Thursday is near.

[11/16/1995] Thursday 16th.

Elections. Then comes the hour of the Apocalypse: Jesus passes through death, eviscerates his tomb, bursts open our appearances, emerges no matter where, no matter when. Every minute is his. (Jean Grosjean. *Apocalypse*, p. 17.)

[11/19/1995] Sunday.

Zéroual's victory has a bitter taste for some. At what price . . . in human lives! Reflections in community on the subject of "charism and situation." Are we just repeating the same things over and over again, or is the experience we are living together the crucible of a new language? We're beginning a book on Little Sister Madeleine of Jesus.[36] People will talk about the "charism of the Little Sisters." The introduction by Jean Vanier shows how close certain charisms are to one other, and how much they gain from interacting. A charism is a lived response.

[11/26/1995] Christ the King: you.

. . . And me: remember me when you come. Soon. Take us—and me—with you. On the phone just now: Philippe's voice right after Jean-Marc's. And this morning: Christian, from Fez.

[12/03/1995] First Sunday of Advent.

In deep thought, Ali wonders why (nearly) all generals and colonels are fat and big.

[12/04/1995] Monday.

In the morning we hear from our neighbors that two corpses are lying on the side of the road to Ain el-Ares. They are two women, mother and daughter maybe! On Friday we will celebrate *insh' Allah* the Immaculate Conception of Mary most holy. Father Amédée's emotional distress is acute—he who receives so many women every day.[37] Brother Luc's is . . . so great that he is silent today.

[12/08/1995] Immaculate Conception.

Guileless MARY, born free.

36. Madeleine Hutin (1898–1989), foundress of the Little Sisters of Jesus (1939), a religious community based on the life and spiritual teachings of Blessed Charles de Foucauld. They started their work in Algeria.

37. He helped Brother Luc in the dispensary.

[12/09/1995] The 9th.

I'm copying for the second time these lines from J. Sommet in *L'honneur de la liberté* ["The Honor of Freedom"], (in the chapter: "Dachau . . . Typhus"): "There I assist at what I call the birth of the Church. It is more a matter of reconstituting a community that gives meaning to each individual's freedom, and that also remains an authentic source of that same freedom, because it does not accept being in a situation of power. [. . .] This is what constitutes a true Church, a society of gratuity and powerlessness, a community without the means of physical or biological resistance, without hidden arms. These men jump in the fray with bare hands. Here we are before a Church that reinvents herself as a place of the heart and of the freedom of people together, each one existing by virtue of the others. [. . .] Such a Church refuses to become a locus of power, of damnation, of constraint imposed on other groups. Father Fessard used to say: 'If the Church does not at times risk her existence as a group and as an institution, I am not sure she is being herself'; and: 'All this power, all this authority is the truth of the Church, but on condition that she exercise it to the point of risking her very existence.'"

True fidelity to the Spirit is a gift in the understanding of a situation, the total commitment of self.

Christian is back, bringing a good piece of news that has arrived from Poland to Rabat: Michal. What's happening with Camille?

[12/12/1995] The 12th.

Does my life offer the Breath a hold over me, in love with You who are coming? Mary: she stands upright in the midst of the wind, free because of You.

[12/13/1995] The 13th.

Yesterday, a booby-trapped car at Ain Naadja: 14 victims and some wounded.

[12/19/1995] The 19th.

Time is not only history; it is the poem being composed as well (J.G.). In the history of Algeria we are almost nothing, but as regards the poem: it is words made man in Bethlehem, in Tibhirine.

With you, one must
expect everything
which could well be
almost nothing at all
great love

One must risk
everything
in the smallest nothings
of every
day

Truly everything
of you still remains
for me to live
here today

Christmas: birth of a passion, beginning of a life on fire, genesis of the vital poem.

[12/21/1995] The 21st.

Since you need barely nothing
the smallest yes
to do the impossible here
take me quickly if you please

12/25 is

Christmas for real

[12/26/1995] The 26th.

Christmas: on the threshold there's a sign: "Come in!"
come and see, says the child
the shelter of the encounter is wide
OPEN
  and I enter
  into RELATION

cuddling in the heart of Brother Henri's cassava plant
the Child smiles and opens his arms to us.

[12/31/1995] Sunday of the Holy Family. 12/31.

Those who wanted to kill the Child are dead, but the Dragon continues to attack his descendants, and I feel threatened in the very spot where, into my adult life, is born the child, the son called out of Egypt. Jesus, I beg you, let me never be separated from you. The child and his mother: let me never desert this place of crucified Love.

1996

[01/01/1996] 01/1.

It's started! Let us run in your footsteps.

[01/02/1996] The 2nd.

At the Eucharist, Christian invited us to keep silent—for one minute!—to hear God formulate for each one of us his desires, which he cannot see realized except by us. I prick up my ears: what does the Breath say?

Breathe on my garden
so that my Beloved can enter into his garden
I enter . . .

Since here you are hard at work in my heart. Ah, first of all: disarm it

and if the thing is not too hard—this whole self of mine—purify me

then I may perhaps be able to help you a little
to LOVE.

Emmanuel Levinas[1] died on Christmas Day.

[01/08/1996] 01/8. Monday.

Jesus baptized: the BELOVED.

1. Emmanuel Levinas (1906–1995), French philosopher of Lithuanian-Jewish ancestry, known for his work related to Jewish philosophy, existentialism, ethics, and ontology.

I remember (from my baptism): Love strong as death

no, the great floods cannot quench love (in my heart), nor rivers sweep it away.

But how little I practice it, whereas you love to the utmost.

Since I must go away—and receive myself again (from your hands): in this Ordinary Time

I return to the source of the Gift: to your heart, where I am the BELOVED . . . in order to be GIVEN AWAY.

Ordinary Time is the time of all new things, since in the risen Jesus, Father, I am Your BELOVED of every instant: inspire me to live from that truth.

In everything: go before me with love. I shall try to let you have your way with me.

For love, Father: that you may be well pleased. Baptism is when love truly is GIVEN. . . .

[01/09/1996] Tuesday.

In Ordinary (Marian) Time.

The dove comes down and rests among the two or three gathered in the Name.

The Breath

wafts us into a silence of peace and impels us to love in the common life.

The gift intervenes and launches us into the adventure of being church here today.

Through the heart cracked open we can—I hope and believe—get a glimpse of the Living God:

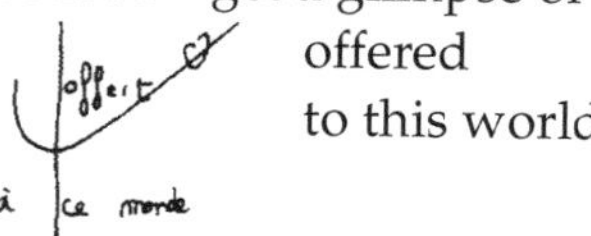

offered

to this world

[01/10/1996] Wednesday.

the moment of singing together quickens us

it's the heart of the task

one must finish well the work
one is given to do
every day
of Eucharistic and
ordinary life.

Come now. Let's be brave: it's You in me who accomplish the act of singing: the act of believing. Jesus! Open my lips.

[01/14/1996] Sunday.

Father Armand (Veilleux)—from Rome—has been with us since Friday: I feel real happiness . . . a Cistercian who draws me toward a more complete self-surrender: into your hands: poor like you, toward the Father.

"The work that is the space of our song": I love this phrase of J.-C. Sagne, and this one too: "Prayer is the great journey of our life. The Holy Spirit makes us follow the way of Jesus in his relationship with the Father." And this one as well: "The human word of Jesus has its source in his filial heart, indwelt by the presence of the Father. It is poverty that lends authority to his word" (re-reading my notes).

After the wash-up, something rather unusual: I answer the phone and hear Mom: I, too, must listen and BEAR, like the Lamb pointed out by John the Baptist today: he bears the sins of the world. Thomas Merton writes: "My monastery is a place in which I disappear from the world as an object of interest in order to be everywhere in it by hiddenness and compassion. In order to be everywhere I have to be No-one."

[01/16/1996] Tuesday.

Behold the lamb, he is here. Soon will be the wedding.

In the hollow of a cassava plant—stronger than murder—it is he: he has been born in our midst,

in order to be offered
in our lives.

[01/17/1996] Wednesday.

Where is the lamb for the ascent?

[01/18/1996] Thursday.

The lamb, and over it the dove, come
to liberate me from the beast, fighting inside me
over my life.

[01/25/1996] Thursday 01/25.

After 24 hours at the Maison Saint-Augustin, where the lavish reception is sweet comfort, here I am this evening, to celebrate our founders, our holy fathers, our brothers of Cîteaux. We are a part of that charism, no doubt about it, our Visitor said. What expectations are implied in this gaze that the Order casts on us. . . . What a responsibility for the poor men we are. After Vigils I looked at the photocopy that finally arrived from Zaire: a passport . . . Camille Makndo Tungila, born in April, 1967.

[01/28/1996] Sunday.

I expressed a wish to Christian when I met him this morning: "No stole on my cowl if I were to die. Such a symbol would be outdated." I have only to let the Spirit complete it: to become a priest of Algeria, still quite recently ordained.

[01/30/1996] Tuesday 30th.

Since I don't have the necessary linguistic or religious knowledge to enter into dialogue with Islam, I feel called simply to listen. And it is God, listened to in the Word he sent, who tells me to listen: to welcome all this strange, very different reality. Even to the point of feeling responsible for it: may the Spirit lead it to the fullness of truth. And, if we can accomplish that journey together, so much the better! And we'll be able to both talk and be silent together along the way.

[02/07/1996] Wednesday 02/7.

Yesterday, a letter from M.-Annick: words that touch me and connect me to others—to the "body of humanity," as Jacques Sommet calls it, whose *L'acte de mémoire* ["The Act of Memory"] I've just read. Last night, during Vigils, I read for all to hear the passage on typhus at Dachau: "The somehow infinite gaze of faithful friendship." And so many other passages should be heard again, for instance: we are not prisoners of history (p. 30). History moves forward through trials to resurrection, through failures to solidarity, through contradictions to communion (p. 73). To accept the reality of an ongoing redemption within a history that is always being put to the test (p. 86). Faith in the resurrection gives the assurance that God keeps the future open even in death (p. 88).

TO LIVE THE RESURRECTION WITHIN A PERSONAL RELATIONSHIP WITH GOD (and)

forgiveness is certainly a resurrection lived between persons.

History is always made together with others, beyond my own time, beyond my little personal space (p. 33). Here is the foundation for the possibility of a new humanity. What interests me is the truth that emerges from of a relation with God within a precise, given experience. The future, for me, is to listen ever anew (p. 48). Poor Clares, present by virtue of the most complete disinterestedness (p. 52).

GOD CAN BE HEARD ONLY IF HE IS LISTENED TO THROUGH EVERY HUMAN BEING (p. 54).

What does the least of men then become for me?

Jesus: SACRIFICIAL UNBOUNDEDNESS.

I saw Dad in his bed, reading: in every flesh, as it expires, a promise is inscribed.

[02/18/1996] Sunday.

29th day of Ramadan. Friday evening, two "rustics" [policemen] assassinated at Tamesguida. And so many others, victims of their own brothers in humanity. Today you say: "Do not resist the wicked. Love your enemies. Pray for them." I re-read my notes on E. Levinas: "I would say that the subject who says 'Here

I am' bears witness to the Infinite. It is this witness, whose truth is neither representational nor perceptual, that produces the revelation of the Infinite. It is through this witness that the very glory of the Infinite glorifies itself. The witness witnesses to what has been said through him."

[02/19/1996] Monday 19th.

Koranic psalmody in the night. It's *'Eid* again. The sky is cloudless, pure. Jean-Pierre is back. The letter Michaël has written Christian is good, beautiful, simple, true. Much violence and bloodshed in the country, again and again. I sowed my second cross somewhere in the garden. Sister M.-E. made it and gave it to me, in the shape of a Franciscan T. I've hung around my neck again the one made by Bernard (of Dombes[2]). When will it be the hour to be sown—beloved in you—at Tibhirine?

Hampâté Bâ's[3] story of his wedding, which we read in the refectory, moves me: the joy of a wedding.

Lent 1996

[02/21/1996] Ash Wednesday.

"But the hour is coming, and is now here, when true adorers will adore the Father in the Breath and the truth, because it is such adorers that the Father seeks."

I relate these words of Yours to those Mohammed said to me last Friday (27th day of Ramadan) when we were working together. They're from the Koran, no doubt, because I had asked him which Word of revelation "spoke" to him most clearly that day. He said: "Let all adore Him [or: prostrate themselves]."

At the Eucharist, Christian also has strong, substantial words, nourishing: "Continuity with last Sunday's gospel . . .

2. Notre-Dame des Dombes, a Cistercian monastery of monks in eastern France, which closed in 2001.

3. Amadou Hampâté Bâ (1901–1991), a writer and ethnologist from Mali.

not to deceive oneself about observances . . . in the presence of the Father—under his gaze—and continuity with Ramadan (taken in tow! why not?)." Mohammed replied: "This Ramadan . . . nothing has happened . . . everything is as usual. . . ." It proposes to us five pillars: Patience, Prayer, Sharing, Pardon and Peace. They coincide with my image of Lent!

[02/22/1996] Thursday.

A feast! Already! St. Peter's Chair. This Lent is *ecclesial*: it's the CHURCH being led into the desert to be nourished there.

[02/26/1996] 02/26.

Driven by the Spirit into the desert: Jesus, conqueror of Evil. He did not fall down and worship.

We, too, are driven by the Spirit into the desert of our retreat, to be won over more radically to your cause: the greater love.

Father Bernard Rérolle is here.

[02/27/1996] The 27th.

The ONE thing that is necessary (in fraternal life: choosing to relish the best part of each one).

ONE in His prayer, our heart must stand at the foot of the Cross

What is necessary is . . . for this *must* to become as necessary to me as *breathing*. May your Breath come to me.

[02/28/1996] The 28th.

Yesterday, a practical exercise: measured breathing. I repeat it and give it a Marian dimension. I receive it as the intimacy of a Breath given to her, to each one of us. Near you: I am. To withdraw to one's "chamber": to the place where worldly eyes have no access, but only the Gaze of the Father who sees in secret. May your Gaze deliver me from all looking at myself, and deliver me from all worry about the opinion others might have of me. Last night, in a dream, I met Dad: yes, it was his face. He turned to me; I took his hand and stroked it. What stays with me is the impression of a luminous suffering that loves and is loved. The communion of the saints is a communion in crucified Love. And this morning Father Bernard Rérolle, while professing Jesus Christ, acknowledged having received from Buddha his intuition of a universal suffering and of a way to avoid being crushed by it.

To carry one's cross: is not this the way?

Yesterday I read a long letter from an Algerian woman whom I met here three years ago and who is a catechumen: joy.

Tonight I read Christian Bobin: "Love comes, love goes. Always in its own time, never in ours. To come, it demands all of heaven, all of the earth, the whole of our language. It could not be contained within the narrowness of only one meaning; it could not even be content with only one form of happiness. Love is freedom. Freedom does not go well with happiness. It goes well with joy. Joy is like a ladder of light in our heart. It leads us much higher than ourselves, much higher that itself: to where there is nothing left to grasp except the ungraspable." (*Éloge du rien* ["In praise of nothingness"])

[02/29/1996] Thursday.

A retreat is a visitation by the Breath given to a particular church. It is for us to understand what it says to us. I don't follow Father Bernard Rérolle when he speaks of the Father without a face. How could Jesus have called him "Abba," even in his very last cry, when that Face seemed to turn away from his trust and no longer to respond to his love? The Father is nothing but FACE.

[03/02/1996] Saturday.

This morning my Lenten reading—Fénelon[4]—seemed to show me the place where I'm to live my life: a meditation on

4. François de Salignac de la Mothe-Fénelon (1651–1715), French Catholic theologian, poet, and writer.

Holy Saturday—buried with Christ in his death. Other than by this death to myself there is no true, decisive, redeeming love. I would be left only with myself.

[03/03/1996)] Sunday.

Moussa says: "Fear of R.?! One shouldn't be afraid except of God." "So, was that father happy here?" "Yes." "So he saw with his own eyes that there's peace here." (We could hear shots from a semi-automatic, and two helicopters hovering over the mountains, and Brother Paul in Medea barely escaped an operation by the armed forces that is said to have left five dead . . .) Moussa was talking of peace not as the world gives it (which is so precarious!) but of another peace that he savors and shares because he lives of it in his own depths. Accompanying Bénédicte as she begins her new job at the hospital: may she experience a real beginning.

[03/04/1996] Monday 03/4.

Today, Camille's 29th birthday, on this feast of Saint Casimir (his original baptismal name, later "deformed" to Camille). "Love one other as *I* have loved you," Jesus says in the Eucharist. He unveils the positive contents of the old commandments, by filling them with Love. Only dying to myself will allow me to enter into this new dimension and commune in the work of the Cross. Abba, not what I want, but what *You* want.

[03/10/1996] Sunday.

Jesus, tired by the journey, is *very simply* sitting there (just like that, without any fuss) at the edge of the well.

March 19th

Saint Joseph. With Bruno and Father Joseph Carmona, who arrived yesterday. Anniversary of my consecration to Mary. Yes,

I continue to choose you, Mary, along with Joseph, in the communion of all saints—and I receive you from Jesus' hands along with the poor and the sinners. With the beloved disciple, I take you to my home. Near you, I am: offered up. In the garden this morning, a good conversation about marriage with Moussa. I'm happy to have presided at the Eucharist. It was as if I heard Joseph inviting me to sing Psalm 100, along with him and the child: "My song is about kindness and justice. . . . I shall walk the way of perfection. When will you come to me? . . . I SHALL WALK with a perfect ♡."

Photos and Facsimiles

Brother Christophe,
photographed by
Claudine Ducolle
(05/21/1994)

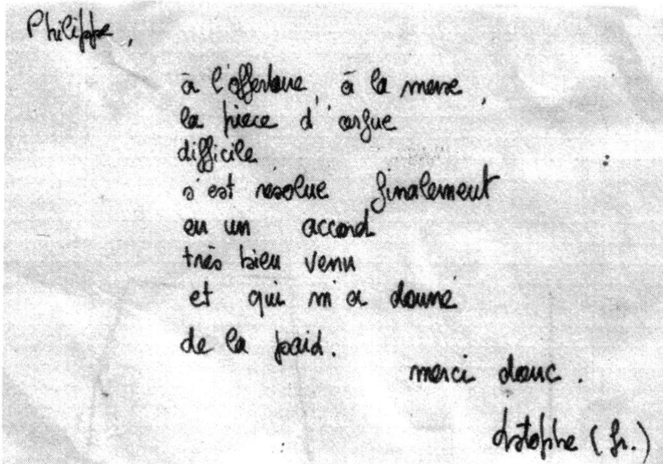

Philippe,

à l'offertoire, à la messe,
la pièce d'orgue
difficile
s'est résolue finalement
en un accord
très bien venu
et qui m'a donné
de la paix.

merci donc.

Christophe (fr.)

Friendly note from Brother Christophe to Brother Philippe of Tamié, after a Mass at the Abbey of Tamié

Ordination card: "If you knew the gift of God" (01/01/1990)

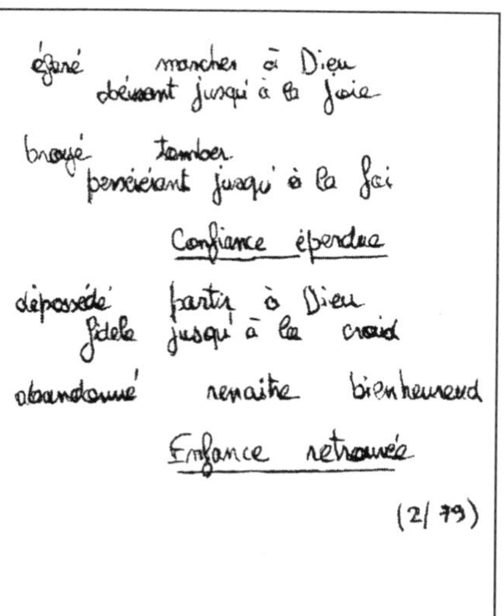

espéré marcher à Dieu
obéissant jusqu'à la joie

broyé tomber
persévérant jusqu'à la foi

Confiance éperdue

dépossédé partir à Dieu
fidèle jusqu'à la croix

abandonné renaître bienheureux

Enfance retrouvée

(2/79)

Unpublished poem (February, 1979)

et ce fut l'écriture ordinaire
obéie grave
secrète et frémissante

du mot de passe : toi
Joie

tout à côté les semis de tomate

et dans mon cœur une joie
bien arrosée

je l'entendais silencieuse se glisser en ma chair et
s'inscrire

dessinée sur les feuillets intimes d'un carnet
de moine usagé

joie toi

Oh mais ça va loin
toi passant par où je suis

tu me ris
tu me traverses
tu me crucifies

c'est écrit de ta main
c'est rempli de lumière
c'est brûlant

c'est prière comme sang répandu c'est pour tous ♡

The password *Toi-Joie* ["You-Joy"], spring 1993

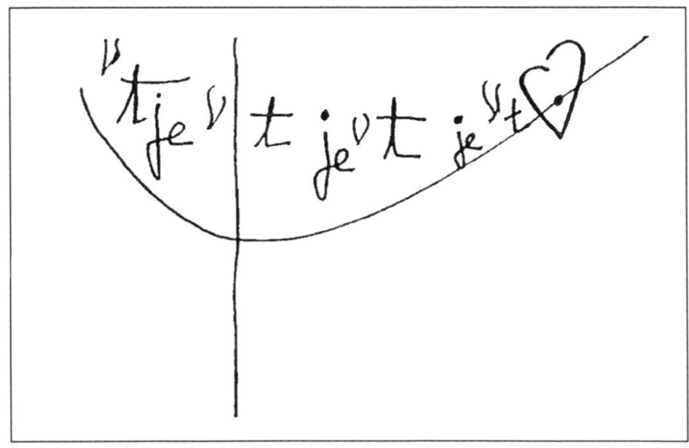

Drawing in the journal (11/05/93)

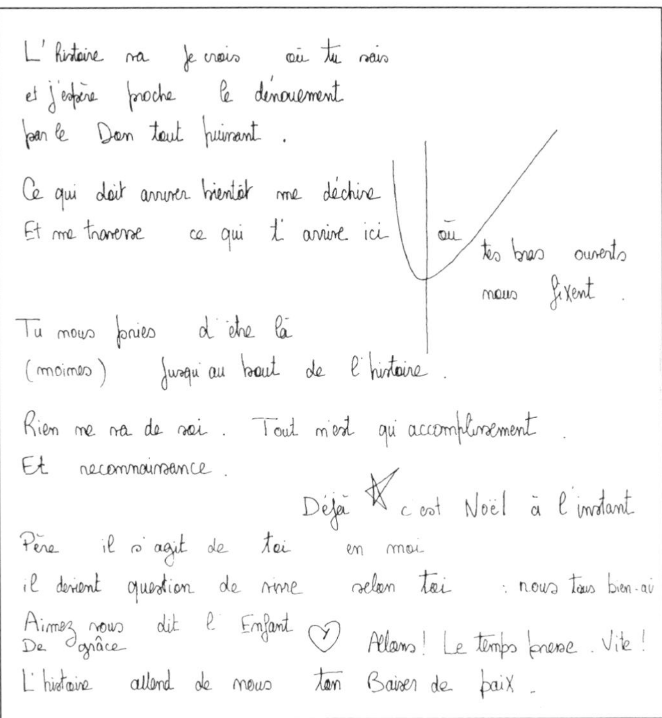

L'histoire va je crois où tu sais
et j'espère proche le dénouement
par le Don tout puissant .

Ce qui doit arriver bientôt me déchire
Et me traverse ce qui t'arrive ici où
tes bras ouverts
nous fixent .

Tu nous pries d'être là
(moines) jusqu'au bout de l'histoire .

Rien ne va de soi . Tout n'est qu'accomplissement .
Et reconnaissance .

Déjà c'est Noël à l'instant

Père il s'agit de toi en moi
il devient question de vivre selon toi : nous tous bien-ai
Aimez nous dit l'Enfant
De grâce
Allons ! Le temps presse . Vite !
L'histoire attend de nous ton Baiser de paix .

Extract from the journal (12/03/93)

Letter to
Brother Didier,
Easter 1995

Didier bien aimé

ta lettre, ta voix, ton coeur
m'ont rejoint à l'Heure de
Jésus
nous aimant
jusqu'au bout

et dans ses mains notre amitié
était remise. Et ce même Jeudi très saint je
recevois de Jean-Paul et Elizabeth : une étole.
Oh je suis encore si loin de vivre dans l'amitié
de ce Mystère. Mais j'ai senti un appel
profond à : obéir (me laisser faire).
Et puis il y a cette croix tombée en terre ...
Tu ne me parles pas de ta santé. Est-ce mieux?
Merci pour ta mémoire d'ami reveillant mon coeur
plus endurci. Mon péché (orgueil - impatiences
et manque d'accueil) s'est fait plus pesant.
Toi tu m'entraînes vers l'AMOUR plus grand.
Je suis heureux de toi, de ces fiançailles
d'amour : plus tu es au Christ
et plus je reçois de toi
et plus je rends grâces
au PERE Bien Aimé.

Je vais preparer un petit air de guitare : ce sera
apres la COMMUNION : musique de PAQUES
je veux jouer pour toi.

Tibhirine le 20/03-96

Lettre adorable de Sophie qu'elle présente un peu pour la réponse ... après PÂQUE.

Chère Maman,

Le Père Carmona venu fêter la St Joseph après avoir accueilli fr. Bruno à l'aéroport m'offre un acheminement plus sûr. Je te glisse quelques mots en réponse à ta lettre du 4/03 tout juste arrivée. Christian descend sur Alger pour une réunion des Supérieurs (religieux/x). Il nous reviendra samedi. Le 31/03 sera vite arrivé mais les élections se feront sans D. Remy qui a renoncé à venir (difficultés avec son passeport estampillé d'un cachet israélien!). Notre archevêque viendra présider l'opération.

Ou plus exactement la co-présider avec l'Esprit Saint. Puisse Christian recevoir force et paix pour continuer à porter sa charge pastorale.

Bruno m'a apporté une lettre très délicate du P. Jean de la Croix. Nous sommes heureux de la présence de Bruno après 5 1/2. La prochaine rencontre du Ribât va nous rappeler de "vieux souvenirs" de l'accueil d'antan: 12 frères annoncés. Inch Allah.

Je m'unis à ta faiblesse: ouverte à son amour plus fort. Essayons d'en être simplement des signes. Sachons reconnaître dans toute personne ce qui en subsiste et qui peut s'unir, communier.

Près de Marie je te suis tout proche et t'embrasse bien affectueusement.

Christophe

Letter to his mother (03/20/96)

Carême 96

في سبيل السّلام

أنا هو me voici

pour l'amour de Dieu PAIX

40 jours

40 nuits

في الفتح

dans l'ouverture

أنا الباب

Je suis la porte

simplement là

près de Marie

disciples de l'AGNEAU

بالرّحمة

en compassion

أنا الرّاعي الصالح

Je suis le bon berger

بالصّبر

en patience

أنا الكرمة الحق

Je suis la vigne véritable

مصلّي

en prière

أنا خبز الحياة

Je suis le pain de vie

Allons ! نذهب

Amour ! محبّة

ma Joie ! سروري

Lenten Cross, 1996

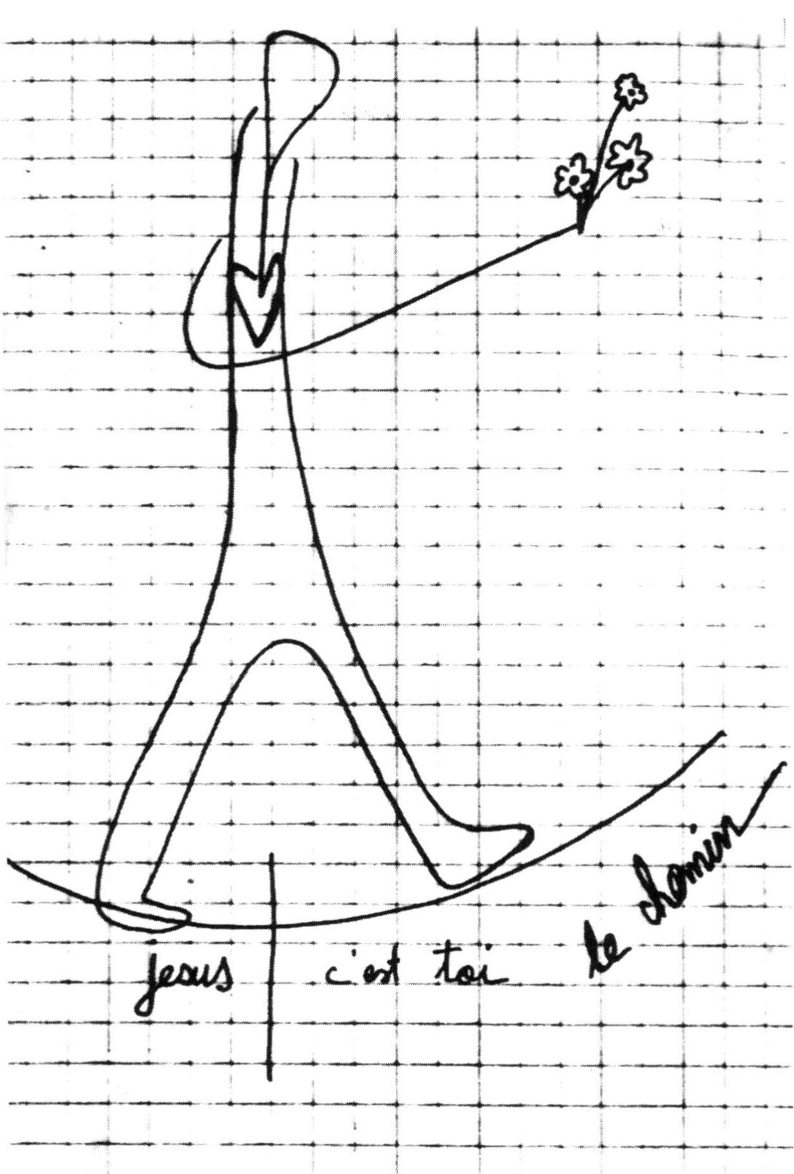
Jesus c'est toi le chemin

Various drawings

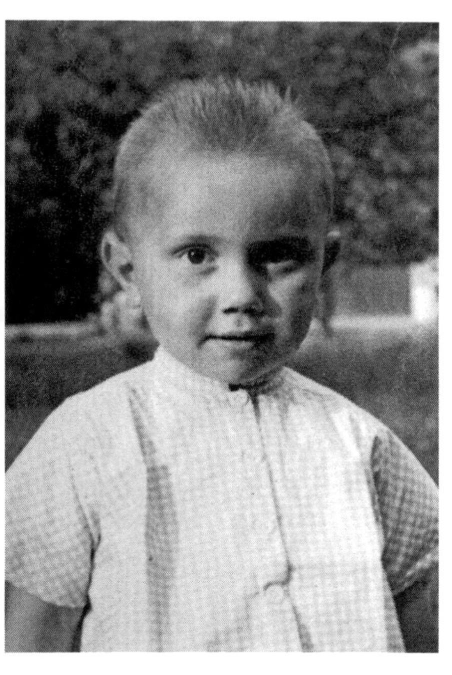

Christophe as a child
and as a teenager

Visit to Tibhirine, 1974

Arrival at Tamié (09/19/74)

The novice at Tamié (April, 1976)

Solemn profession (11/01/80)

Working in the woods at Tamié

Christophe as guestmaster at Notre-Dame des Dombes, 1986

Departure from Tamié to go help out at the Abbey of Notre-Dame des Dombes (01/26/86)

At Tibhirine with Amédée, Célestin, and Jean-Pierre

At Tibhirine with Michel, Luc, Bruno, Christian, and Célestin

Surrounded by nephews and nieces who had come to Tibhirine for his ordination to the priesthood (01/01/90)

At Tibhirine with his neighbors

In front of the monastery of Our Lady of Atlas (Tibhirine)

Celebrating Mass at Tamié, where he had gone for the priestly ordination of his friend Brother Philippe, by Bishop Marcel Perrier (05/21/94)

The community of Our Lady of Atlas during the regular visitation by Dom Armand Veilleux (01/20/96)

A few days before the abduction, with Célestin, Bruno, and some neighbors (03/20/96)

Paschal Cross, made at Tamié by Brother Christophe